PRESCHOOL/KINDERGARTEN

INSTANT LESSONS

For Little Learners

From Your Friends At The MAILBOX® Magazine

About This Book

Do any of these situations sound familiar?

- That art project didn't take as long as you thought it would. There are still 15 minutes before lunch.
- You have to leave your assistant in charge while you take an urgent phone call.
- Madeline's mom forgot to send in the sugar. No cooking lesson today!

If you've ever needed a lesson in a hurry, then this book is for you! It's been designed to provide you with valuable and creative activities you can do on the spur of the moment. The first seven sections describe teaching ideas that require no materials at all, or only basic items you'll have handy in your early childhood classroom—such as paper, tape, or a ball. Look in these sections to find ideas for math, language, movement, science, games, and more.

The remaining sections are divided by the materials and manipulatives commonly found in a preschool or kindergarten classroom. Just flip through the pages and you'll see a wealth of ideas for quick-and-easy activities with craft sticks, beanbags, paper plates, yarn—even children's shoes and the chairs they sit in!

You'll never have to worry about filling a few extra minutes again! And these ideas are so simple and easy to implement, they're perfect for your assistant or a substitute to carry out. With *Instant Lessons For Little Learners* at your fingertips, you'll always be prepared!

PRESCHOOL/KINDERGARTEN

INSTANT LESSONS

For Little Learners

From Your Friends At **The MAILBOX®** Magazine

Editors:
Ada Goren
Angie Kutzer
Mackie Rhodes

Artists:
Jennifer Tipton Bennett
Cathy Spangler Bruce
Pam Crane
Clevell Harris
Susan Hodnett
Sheila Krill
Mary Lester
Rob Mayworth
Rebecca Saunders
Donna K. Teal

©1997 by THE EDUCATION CENTER, INC.
All rights reserved except as here noted.
ISBN# 1-56234-177-4

Manufactured in the United States
10 9 8 7 6 5 4 3 2 1

TABLE OF CONTENTS

Paper and Crayons 74

Jump Ropes 78

Pipe Cleaners 80

Crackers 82

Beads and Laces 84

Puzzles...................................... 86

Two-Sided Counters 88

Paper Plates............................... 90

Beans 92

Nature Items............................... 94

Play Dough.................................. 96

Dominoes 100

Rubber Stamps 102

Toy Vehicles............................. 104

Chairs 106

Paper and Scissors 108

Buttons 110

Plastic Food 112

Paper Lunch Bags....................... 114

Language 5

Math 13

Science 21

Dramatic Play 29

Movement 37

Songs, Fingerplays, and Poems 45

Games........................ 53

Craft Sticks 62

Pom-Poms 66

Rhythm Instruments 68

Straws 70

Hoops............................ 72

Index Cards 116

Clothespins 118

Geoboards 120

Linking Cubes 122

Animal Figures 124

Pasta 126

Balls 128

Wooden Blocks 130

Magnetic Letters and Numbers 132

Cotton Balls and Cotton Swabs ... 136

Sticky Dots 138

Teddy-Bear Counters 140

Plastic Dishes and Pans 142

Cookies 144

Paper and Tape 146

Chalk and Chalkboards 148

Sticky Notes 150

The Classroom Calendar 152

Duplos® 154

Cookie Cutters 156

Shoes 158

Seashells 160

Pattern Blocks 162

Books 164

Sand 166

Beanbags 168

Bubbles and Blowers 172

Paper Cups 174

Markers 176

Dice 178

Yarn 180

Newspapers and Magazines 182

Plastic Links 184

Dress-Up Clothes and Props 186

Stencils 188

Crepe-Paper Streamers 190

LANGUAGE

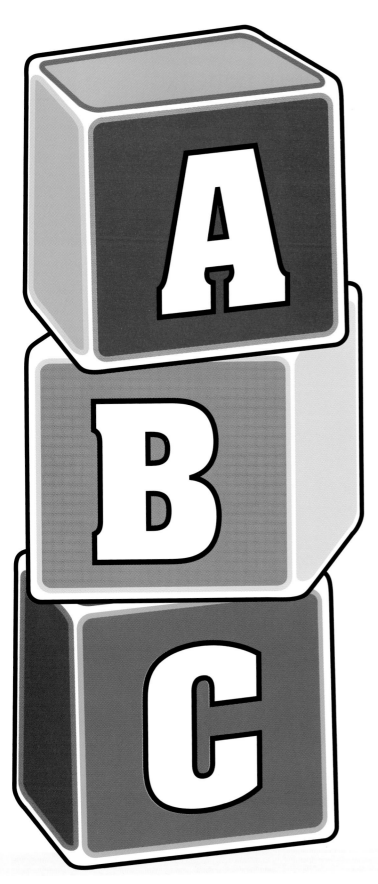

LANGUAGE

ABCs—and lots of other language skills—
are as easy as 1-2-3 with these
spur-of-the-moment activities!

ideas contributed by Rachel Castro, Linda Gordetsky, Mary Kathryn Martell, and Virginia Zeletzki

Tell Me All About It

Youngsters will generate lots of descriptive language with this activity. Seat your students in a circle and choose any object in your classroom. Hand the object to one child and ask him to name the object and tell one thing about it. For example, a child might say, "This block is made of wood." Then have him pass the object to the child beside him. Encourage that child to repeat the statement of the first child and add a description of his own. For example, the second child might say, "This block is made of wood and it's smooth." Have the children continue to pass the object until the child who receives the object can't think of another descriptive word or phrase. Then give that child a new object and begin again.

Mystery

Invite your little ones to play detective as you give a description of a mystery object or person. For example, if you choose a lollipop as the mystery item, you might give clues such as "It is round," "It is sweet," and "It has a stick." Use tally marks on the chalkboard or a sheet of chart paper to keep track of how many clues you must give before someone guesses correctly. Play again and see if the group can lower their score.

This pillow is red and it's square and it's soft...

A lollipop!

Flashlight I Spy

All you need is a flashlight for this fun game. To prepare, teach children the chant below. Then dim the classroom lights and hand the flashlight to one child. Have the class recite the rhyme. Then give the child a clue, such as "I spy something that tells time." Ask the child to shine the flashlight on the object he thinks you're describing.

For variety—and to help students practice identification skills—give clues about the color, shape, or beginning sound of the object's name ("I spy something that begins with *C* and tells time"). Continue the game until every child has had a turn to shine the flashlight on an object.

Although inside it's very dark,
And I can hardly see,
If I look closely, I might find
What you describe to me.

Under.

Find It

If you're searching for a way to help youngsters understand positional words, try this activity. Have one child step away from the group while you hide an object somewhere in the classroom. Then—in the same fashion as the old game You're Hot/You're Cold—give the child clues to follow in order to find the object. But instead of using the terms *hot* and *cold,* use only positional words—such as *near, far, on, under, left, right, inside,* and so on—to direct the child's search. Once the child has located the object, let him hide it for the next searcher.

Listen-Up Lineup

Turn lineup time into learning time with this activity. Ask the designated line leader to listen to your directions as she puts the other children in line. Give directions using positional words, such as "Put Amy *between* Mark and Jonah. Put Mario *in front of* Allyssa. Put Donnie *behind* A. J." If a child has difficulty understanding a command, invite her classmates to help her. The next time the class lines up, invite a different child to complete the Listen-Up Lineup.

Put Amy between Mark and Jonah.

Rrrring!

Do You Hear What I Hear?

Try this twist on a tried-and-true activity to perk up your students' listening skills. Ask your students to listen carefully as you say a list of words that name household objects. Tell them that when they hear an object that makes a noise, they should imitate that noise. For example, your list might sound like this: "Chair, table, rug, telephone…" When children hear the word *telephone,* they should respond by imitating the ringing of a phone. Sounds like fun!

Nursery Rhyme Recitation

Encourage your youngsters to develop their speaking skills with this activity modeled after the traditional game of London Bridge. Choose two students to join hands and create a "bridge" as in the original game. Invite the other children to line up and parade under the bridge one at a time as the class sings the following song. At the end of each verse, instruct the two children forming the bridge to catch a child between their arms. Then have that child recite a nursery rhyme of his choice. Continue the game until everyone who wishes to recite a rhyme has had an opportunity.

(sung to the tune of "London Bridge")

Nursery rhymes are lots of fun,
Lots of fun, lots of fun.
Nursery rhymes are lots of fun,
Can you tell one?

Hickory dickory dock...

The turtle colored his shell all different colors.

Tell A Tale

Sharpen your children's creativity and ability to connect ideas with this storytelling activity. Seat the children in a circle and choose any two objects in your classroom. Give the two objects to one child and ask her to begin a story about the two items. Have her pass the items to the child beside her; then invite that child to add to the story. Continue around the circle until every child has had an opportunity to add to the story. If desired, tape-record the children's story and write it out later. Copy the written version for each child to take home.

Alphabet Names

Little ones will enjoy identifying beginning sounds when their own names are involved. First teach youngsters the chant below. At the end of the chant, call out each letter of the alphabet, either in order or randomly. Instruct each child to call out his name when he hears the letter that begins his name.

A-B-C-D-E-F-G...
Can you say your name for me?

Limbo Language

Students will be bending over backward to try this activity! Ask two volunteers to hold the ends of a yardstick as they would for a game of limbo. Begin with the yardstick high enough so that children can comfortably walk beneath it. Ask the other children to line up one behind another on one side of the yardstick. As each child approaches the stick, have him tell you a word and name its beginning sound. For example, a child might say, "Dog begins with a *D.*" Or—if you focus on one letter sound at a time—have all the children name a word with that letter's sound. After the child successfully names the word and/or sound, have him walk under the stick. After everyone has passed under the stick once, have the two volunteers lower the stick slightly and play another round. Continue the game until all the children are slithering under the stick.

Vary the game to have children name rhyming words or opposites, or to identify colors or shapes of familiar objects.

Rhyming Bee

Your youngsters may be too young for an old-fashioned spelling bee, but a game of Rhyming Bee will have them all abuzz! To play this cooperative game, designate one area of the room as the hive and have students line up one behind another across the room from it. Explain to your students that they are all bees, and you are the Queen (or King) Bee. To get into the hive, each bee must name a word that rhymes with the word you say. Say a word and encourage each bee, in turn, to name a word from that rhyming family. As each bee names a rhyming word, she may go into the hive. At the point when a child cannot think of a rhyme, stop and count how many bees are in the hive. Then invite all the bees in the hive to fly out and join the end of the line of bees. Begin again with a new word for the child at the front of the line.

If desired, keep track of students' success by jotting down the number of bees that get into the hive during each round. When time is up, invite your little bees to swarm around and take a look at their highest score.

Rhyme Go-Round

For more rhyming review, try this circle-time rhyming contest. Seat all your students in a circle. Have a designated child stand behind one of the seated children. Stand in the center of the circle and say a word. The standing child and the child seated in front of her both try to say a word that rhymes with your word. If the standing child is the first to say a rhyming word, she goes on to stand behind the next child in the circle. If the seated child is the first to say a rhyming word, he gets up and stands behind the next child in the circle, and the child who was standing takes his seat. Continue the game as long as desired.

Vary the game by asking students to identify beginning sounds or opposites.

Opposite Simon Says

This variation on the game of Simon Says is a fun way to reinforce the concept of opposites. Begin by playing the part of Simon yourself. Give a command to the children, such as "Simon says sit down." Then command children to do the opposite action—"Simon says stand up." Continue for a few rounds, giving commands for different opposite pairs. Then give more advanced children a chance to play the part of Simon. Have a volunteer whisper his commands in your ear first to make sure they are opposites. Then let him give the commands for the children to perform.

Opposites Around The Circle

Teach little ones this circle-time song to help them learn about opposites. After singing the song together, go around the circle and invite each child to name a pair of opposites.

(sung to the tune of "Twinkle, Twinkle, Little Star")

Opposites are all around.
The opposite of up is down.
In and out and black and white,
The opposite of day is night.
Opposites are not the same.
Are there opposites you can name?

Tall and short.

Hot and cold.

MATH

Use this collection of activities to spice up each day with math. The skills are all here—from number sense, to positional words, to patterns, and more. So mix these mathematical ingredients together and cook up an instant batch of fun!

ideas contributed by Barbara Backer, Rachel Castro, Joyce Montag, Vicki Pacchetti, Ellen Weiss, and Virginia Zeletzki

Count The Beats

Claps and taps are all you need to help your children practice counting. Tell students to listen carefully as you clap or use a pencil, a ruler, or another handy object to tap a hard surface from one to ten times. Encourage volunteers to count aloud the number of claps or taps. For a variation, say a numeral; then direct your children to clap the correct number of times. Continue until interest wanes.

Top Ten Lists

Reinforce the number concept of *ten* with this idea. Divide your class into small groups. Give each group a topic (some suggested topics are listed below to get you started). Write each assigned topic on a separate piece of chart paper; then list ten of the group's examples that relate to the designated topic. Make sure to number each example; then emphasize the numerals in some way: use a different-colored marker from the text's color, circle them, or make them bold. Invite each group to illustrate its list. Compile the finished lists to make a big book for the reading center. This suggestion definitely scores a perfect ten!

Types Of Drinks
1. Kool-Aid®
2. soda pop
3. water
4. orange juice
5. tea
6. coffee
7. hot chocolate
8. milk
9. lemonade
10. milkshakes

by: Katie, Eric, Tyrone

Healthful Activities	Things To Do In Winter
Fruits	Animals
Vegetables	Books
Pizza Toppings	Kinds Of Clothing
Types Of Drinks	Names Of Restaurants

Face-Off!

Introduce your class to a "fun-tastic" feud with this variation of the popular game show. Divide your class into two teams. Cut out two construction-paper circles (buzzers) and tape one to each end of a desktop or tabletop. To play the game, direct one member of each team to stand at a buzzer. Announce the word, "Before," or "After," and then a numeral from one to ten. Give the first child who taps her buzzer the opportunity to answer. If she is correct, give her team a point. If she is incorrect, give the other player a chance to answer. Play continues, alternating between teams until a correct answer is given. Then call up two more players for another face-off.

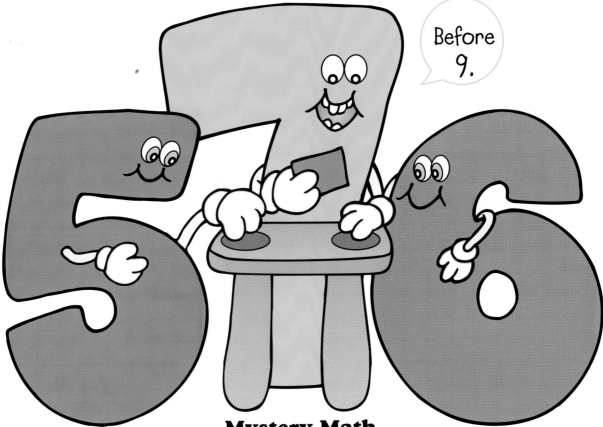

Before 9.

Mystery Math

Put your youngsters on the case to discover the identities of these mystery numbers by using their numeral-recognition and counting skills. Divide your class into pairs, designating one partner in each pair as the Detective and the other partner as the Clue Giver. Have the Clue Giver use his index finger to "write" a numeral on the Detective's back; then have the Detective guess the numeral.

For a more difficult case, have the Clue Giver choose a number from one to ten, then draw a matching set of shapes on the Detective's back. Challenge the Detective to count the number of shapes, then write the matching numeral on the Clue Giver's back. Have the pair discuss the results. Did they crack the case?

The Right Course

Set little ones on the right course for learning positional words with this energetic activity. Make an obstacle course in your room by positioning several items that are handy—such as a table, yardstick, hoop, and chair—randomly around the area. Leave as much space as possible between items. Direct your students to line up and follow you around the course while singing this positional-word song.

*(sung to the tune of
"Go In And Out The Window")*

I'm crawling *under* the table.
I'm crawling *under* the table.
I'm crawling *under* the table,
So come and follow me.

*Repeat the song, substituting
the following sentences:*
    I'm stepping *over* the yardstick….
    I'm walking *around* the chair….
    I'm jumping *through* the hoop….

Following Directions

Use this instant activity to give your youngsters more practice with directional words. Select a volunteer to be It. Instruct It to give a classmate a directional command using another object or person in the room. For example, It might say, "Stand *near* Sam," or "Sit *under* the art table." After the classmate follows the command, he becomes the next It. For variety, play outdoors or in a gym so that all of the students can follow the directions together. *Above, under, around, through;* we know our direction words—do you?

Swing Your Partner

Strengthen your little ones' understanding of the concepts *front, back,* and *beside* by square-dancing. Invite pairs of volunteers to listen and follow directions as you chant the phrases below. Pause after each question to give the pairs a chance to answer. After the rhyme, it's back to square one—to switch partners for another round of fun!

With your partner
Form a line.
Who's *ahead?*
Who's *behind?*

Change positions;
Quickly act.
Who's *in front?*
Who's *in back?*

Stand *next to*
Your pal, like so.
Who's *beside* you?
Do you know?

Leapin' Lily Pads!

Youngsters will get a jump on addition readiness by dramatizing this froggy poem. To prepare, place ten carpet squares in a row in front of your class. Start the skit by having one volunteer squat, to resemble a frog, on the first carpet square. Chant the first verse of the rhyme below. During the third line of this verse, tap another volunteer to squat on the second carpet square. As the class counts in the last line of each verse, each frog hops in place when his number is called. When ten frogs are on the lily pads, start over with new volunteers. Ribbet, ribbet!

One little frog on a pad having fun
Wanted more frogs to join her in the sun.
Look who's swimming over from the shore.
Now it's time to add one more:
1—2.

Two little frogs on their pads having fun
Wanted more frogs to join them in the sun.
Look who's swimming over from the shore.
Now it's time to add one more:
1—2—3.

(Continue the rhyme, with three to nine in the first line, until all ten frogs are included.)

Left Or Right?

Turn a routine daily walk into a toss-up by using a coin to determine which way to go. Each time your class arrives at a corner, have a different volunteer toss a coin. If the coin lands on heads, the class takes a right at the corner. If the coin lands on tails, the class takes a left at the corner. Little ones will be anxious to see where they'll wind up when the toss becomes impossible to follow. If desired, keep a list of destinations reached during these chancy walks.

Comparing Heights

Help children harvest their seriation skills in this "classmate patch." Have a volunteer stand in front of the group; then select another child to be the Farmer. Ask all the children to stand up. As the class sings the song below, the Farmer picks a classmate who is taller (or shorter) than the volunteer; then that classmate stands beside the volunteer. The Farmer then looks for a classmate who is taller (or shorter) than the second child and so on until the end of the song. After the song, compare the "picked" children's heights, and encourage the Farmer to rearrange their order if necessary. Then "plant" the children back in the classmate patch, select a new Farmer and volunteer, and reap the seriation learning!

(sung to the tune of "The Pawpaw Patch")

Can you find someone who's taller [shorter]?
Can you find someone who's taller?
Can you find someone who's taller,
Somewhere in this classmate patch?

Pickin' the classmates,
Puttin' 'em in order.
Pickin' the classmates,
Puttin' 'em in order.
Pickin' the classmates,
Puttin' 'em in order.
Up in front of the
classmate patch.

A Feet Feat

Step right into this quick measurement activity. Send each of your students on a search to find an item in your classroom that's *longer, shorter,* or *the same size as* her foot. Once she finds an item, direct her to come back to the circle to share and compare her find to those of her classmates. Afterward have the children return the objects to their appropriate places.

Then model how to measure using the non-standard, heel-to-toe method. Challenge youngsters to use their feet to measure the distance from one side of the room to the other (or some other appropriate distance). Start steppin'!

Jump, Frog, Jump!

Invite your little froggies to visit the local lily pad for more measurement fun. Mark a starting line on your floor with chalk or tape. Place a carpet square (lily pad) a short distance away from the line. On your cue have two volunteers jump from the starting line toward the lily pad. Have the rest of the class compare their jumps and state the results using measurement terms, such as *longer, shorter, farther, closer,* etc.

For added fun, make this activity into a relay game. Go to a larger playing area and mark another starting line there. Place the lily pad at the other end of the playing area. Divide your class into two or three small teams; then help each team form a line behind the starting line. To play this game, the first frog in each line leaps as far as he can toward the pad. The second frog in each line races to the first frog's landing spot, then leaps from there. Play continues until one frog from each team reaches the lily pad. Count to see how many leaps it took each team to reach the pad.

People Patterns

Patterns become very concrete when students use themselves as examples in this activity. Position a small group of volunteers to form a pattern, such as *stand, sit, stand, sit, stand.* Ask the rest of the class to determine the pattern; then call more volunteers, one at a time, to extend and complete the pattern. Repeat the activity several times with new poses. Then challenge the first two or three children in a new group to make up their own pattern of poses for the group to follow. Continue until every child has had a turn to create a people pattern.

Count It Out

This quick activity keeps youngsters counting and requires only a beanbag. Have your class sit in a circle on the floor. To start the game, have a volunteer choose and state a number from one to ten. Hand him the beanbag and direct him to start passing it around the circle. The children count aloud as they pass the beanbag the designated number of times. For example, if the volunteer chooses the number four, the beanbag is passed to four children. When it gets to the fourth child, have her stand. Then direct the children to keep passing the beanbag around the circle, having every fourth child stand until there is only one student left sitting. That student gets to announce the next number for the next round of counting and passing. 1–2–3…I hope it lands on me!

SCIENCE

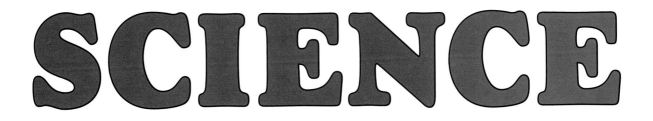

SCIENCE

Ignite some learning excitement with these on-the-spot science activities that stimulate youngsters' skills in observation, investigation, experimentation, demonstration, classification, and imagination!

ideas contributed by Rachel Castro, Suzanne Moore, and Vicki Pacchetti

A Sound In The Silence

When youngsters play this game, they'll sharpen both their listening and reasoning skills. Gather a collection of different (unbreakable) objects in which each item makes a distinct noise when dropped on the ground—such as a paper clip, block, ruler, metal spoon, and book. Then have youngsters listen closely as you drop each item from your collection on the floor. After the demonstration, ask students to cover their eyes and sit very quietly. Drop one item on the floor; then retrieve the item and hide it behind your back. Invite a volunteer to identify the item. Then continue the game with a different item and volunteer. Shhh! Do you hear what I hear?

Shadow On The Wall

Shed some light on the topic of shadows with this idea. To begin, explain to youngsters that a shadow is created when light is blocked by an object. A shadow can appear large or small according to the distance of that object from the light source. Turn on your overhead projector; then invite each student, in turn, to experiment with his hand shadows and their sizes. Teach youngsters this song to reinforce the size comparisons of shadows.

Shadow
(sung to the tune of "Dreidel, Dreidel, Dreidel")

Shadow, shadow, shadow,
I see you on the wall.
And when I move my hands close,
I see you getting small.
Shadow, shadow, shadow,
I see you on the wall.
And when I move my hands far,
You get so big and tall!

Peekaboo Projections

Illuminate students' observational skills while giving them some valuable visual memory practice. To prepare, use one or two file folders to screen the display surface of an overhead projector. Place three or four items with easy-to-identify shapes—such as a pair of scissors, a pencil, a safety pin, and a clothespin—on the projector; then turn on the projector. Encourage youngsters to look at and silently identify the names of the items being projected. After a brief period, turn off the projector; then ask a volunteer to name the items she observed. If she has difficulty recalling all the items, allow her to call on a classmate for help. Then turn on the projector so that she can check her responses. Peekaboo! I thought I saw you!

Vivacious Vibrations

Send some good vibrations to your students with this sound idea. To prepare, squeeze the hook of a metal coat hanger inward so that it forms a loop (for safety); then tie a separate length of yarn to each rounded end of the inverted hanger. Have a child wrap one loose yarn end around one index finger, then do the same with the other yarn end and index finger. Direct him to place his fingers in his ears; then invite a volunteer to tap the hanger with several items made of different materials—such as a wooden pencil, a metal spoon, and a plastic marker. Ask the first child to describe what he experienced—the sound and feeling of the vibrating hanger. Then repeat the procedure until each child has had the opportunity to use the hanger. It's a metallic moment with a sound principle!

Sorting Stones

If a nice, sunny day finds your class with some extra time, here's a great way to absorb a bit of sunshine and some sorting practice. Take your class outdoors on a rock hunt, bringing along a roll of masking tape and a permanent marker. Ask each child to find one rock specimen to donate to a class collection. Write each child's name on a piece of tape to label her find. While outdoors—or back inside the classroom—invite youngsters to sort the collection of rocks by color, size, weight, texture, or even sparkle appeal. For interest and fun, this is a rock-solid idea!

Classy Clouds

This cloudy-day activity will give way to bright and sunny imaginations! On a cloudy—but otherwise nice—day, gather a supply of clipboards, paper, and pencils or black crayons; then take youngsters out for some creative cloud watching. After finding a spacious, open area, invite each child to spend a few moments watching the clouds. If desired, invite youngsters to describe some of their real and imaginary observations. Then ask each child to illustrate her observations on a sheet of paper attached to a clipboard. Have her write/dictate a description of her drawings. Then, return to the classroom and invite each child to share her picture with the class. Whether in puffs or wisps, these clouds have class.

Ramp Runners

Delight youngsters with this fun and simple experiment on distance and speed. Use a removable bookshelf, a big book, a box lid, or a large building block along with a stack of blocks or books to create a ramp. Invite a child to roll a toy vehicle down the ramp, then measure its distance with a length of yarn. Raise or lower the height of the ramp; then repeat the experiment. Did the vehicle travel any farther this time? Did it move faster or slower? After several trials with different ramp angles, lead youngsters in a discussion about their results. Ready to roll?

A Hair-Raising Discovery

Little ones will get a charge out of discovering static electricity. Explain to youngsters that when conditions are favorable—such as on a cold, dry, winter day—they can generate their own form of electricity called *static electricity*. On such a day, invite students to slide their feet across a carpeted area, then to touch various objects to see if a small shock is produced. What happens when they touch metal? Wood? Plastic? One another?

To further reinforce the concept of static electricity, electrically charge a plastic margarine-tub lid by rubbing it back and forth on a child's hair or on a knit sweater being worn by yourself or a child. Then place the lid just above a child's head so that his hair lifts up toward the lid. Explain that the charge in the lid attracts and pulls hair toward it. Guide youngsters to understand that both people and things can generate electricity. Now, that's a real hair-raiser!

Germs On The Go

Here's a neat way to reinforce how germs travel from person to person. Simply hide a piece of rolled tape in the palm of your hand; then explain that germs can be passed by touching one another. Ask a child to shake your hand. As you hold the child's hand, pass the tape into her hand. Then have the child show her classmates the tape—or germ—that you passed to her. Inform youngsters that hand washing is one way to get rid of germs. Teach students this song to make this brief lesson on hygiene really stick.

(sung to the tune of "Three Blind Mice")

Wash your hands.
Wash your hands.
Before you eat.
Before you eat.
The germs on your hands can really stick.
So wash them away so you don't get sick.
Use soap and water to do the trick.
Wash your hands.

Feel The Beat

Does your heart start pounding when you find yourself with unexpected time on your hands? Then why not slip in a quick lesson about the heartbeat? To begin, ask youngsters to feel their heartbeats, then share their observations. Afterward have the students stand and run in place for a short period of time. Ask them to feel their heartbeats again and comment on their findings. Did their heartbeats get faster? Teach youngsters this song to reinforce the impact that exercise has on their heart rates.

(sung to the tune of "Row, Row, Row Your Boat")

Thump, thump goes my heart
When I sit and rest.
It beats so slow,
I hardly know
It's beating in my chest.

Ba-bump, ba-bump goes my heart
When I run and play.
It beats so fast—
But will it last
When I sit down to stay?

Naming Baby

Grow youngsters' animal vocabulary with this activity. Write a student-generated list of animals on a large sheet of paper. Then teach the class this song, replacing the bold-face word with a different animal each time the song is repeated. Encourage students to use the appropriate word to complete the last line of the song.

(sung to the tune of "London Bridge")

What do you call a baby **cat**?
Baby **cat**? Baby **cat**?
What do you call a baby **cat**?
It's called a [kitten]!

It's Covered!

Here's a topic worth covering when you have a few spare moments—animal coverings! Guide youngsters to name the different body coverings found on animals—fur, feathers, scales, and skin. Then invite them to name a few different animals from each group. Reinforce their learning with the song below. After singing the song, call out one of the covering categories; then ask a volunteer to name an animal that fits the category. Continue as student interest or time dictates. No more worry about spare time—it's covered!

(sung to the tune of "Oats, Peas, Beans")
Fur or feathers, scales or skin.
Fur or feathers, scales or skin.
Each animal is all covered in
Fur or feathers, scales or skin.

Perfect Prints

Comparison and categorization practice are right at youngsters' fingertips with this idea. To make a perfect fingerprint, ask a child to rub his fingertip over pencil scribblings on a sheet of paper. Then have him press his finger onto the sticky side of a piece of transparent tape. Affix the tape to a square of white construction paper labeled with the child's name. Invite youngsters to compare their fingerprints; then have them sort the prints by the formations they create—whorls, arches, or loops. It's all here in prints!

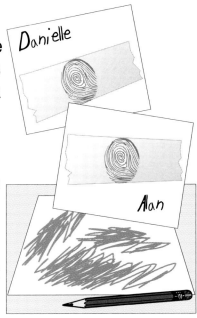

Joint Adventures

Lead youngsters in a joint investigation to discover how different parts of their bodies move. To begin, explain that many body parts are connected at *joints*. These joints are needed so that the body can move. Point out some jointed body parts—such as the elbows, wrists, fingers, knees, ankles, shoulders, and hips. Then invite volunteers to demonstrate some ways different body parts move. For instance, a child might move her hand up and down, side to side, and all around. Or she might move her hips forward and backward and side to side. After the demonstrations, name actions for your class to perform with specific jointed body parts. This is one joint adventure that will be quite moving!

28

DRAMATIC PLAY

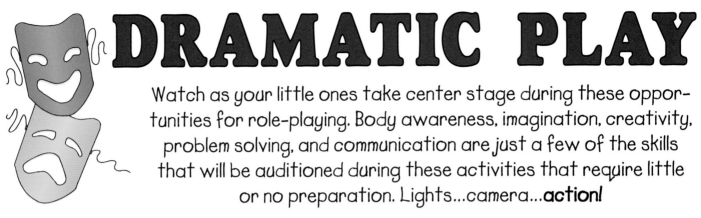

DRAMATIC PLAY

Watch as your little ones take center stage during these opportunities for role-playing. Body awareness, imagination, creativity, problem solving, and communication are just a few of the skills that will be auditioned during these activities that require little or no preparation. Lights...camera...**action!**

ideas contributed by Rachel Castro, Linda Gordetsky, and Carrie Lacher

Animal Antics

Youngsters will love trying to stump their classmates in this guessing game. Help your class form a circle. Have a volunteer stand in the center of the circle. To start the game, he says, "Have you ever seen an animal do this?" then proceeds to imitate an animal action of his choice. Have the rest of the students take turns guessing an animal that performs the action. Invite the child who guesses correctly to switch places with the child in the center of the circle. If no one has a correct guess, have the child in the center of the circle continue with another animal. Be sure to point out that more than one animal hops (swims, flies, etc.), so there can be more than one correct answer!

On The Move

Want more animal-imitating activities? Try this song to get your wild animals on the move. When these verses get old, challenge your youngsters to come up with some new ones of their own. Got your fur, feathers, and fins ready? Let's move!

(sung to the tune of "The Farmer In The Dell")

Hop like a rabbit.
Hop like a rabbit.
Here, there, and everywhere
Hop like a rabbit.

(Repeat with the following verses)
Wiggle like a worm…
Crawl like a spider…
Fly like a bird…
Gallop like a horse…
Swim like a fish…

A Day On The Farm

Take your children on an imaginary trip to the farm as you sing this song and mimic the actions. Before singing each verse for the first time, discuss the action and the tools or supplies needed to complete the chore. Then engage your little farmhands in a hard day's work 'til the cows come home.

(sung to the tune of "Here We Go 'Round The Mulberry Bush")

This is the way we feed the chicks,
Feed the chicks, feed the chicks.
This is the way we feed the chicks
On Old MacDonald's farm.

(Repeat with the following verses)
This is the way we gather eggs…
This is the way we milk the cow…
This is the way we clean the barn…
This is the way we slop the pigs…
This is the way we shear the sheep…
This is the way we ride the horse…
This is the way we plow the field…
This is the way we plant the seeds…

Fact Or Fiction?

Here's a quick dramatic-play activity that promotes critical-thinking skills as children sort through fact and fiction. Direct students to walk around in a circle. As they walk, instruct the children to listen closely to your statements about a variety of animals. Explain to the students that if they hear a true statement, they should stop walking and pretend to be the animal described. If they think the statement is false, they should resume or continue walking. Keep the statements on the appropriate level for your group. Some examples might be, "Pigs have wings. Butterflies swim. Cats have kittens. Horses have two legs." Continue this fact-finding mission until interest wanes.

If…

Keep the animal theme rolling with this dramatic-play activity that requires a little problem solving. Ask your students a question, such as "What animal are you if you eat a carrot?" or "What animal are you if you have a trunk?" Have the children answer by pretending to be the animal described. For a challenge and more variety, ask a few questions with more than one possible answer—such as "What animal are you if you lay eggs?" Hmmm…

Are You A Robot Or A Rag Doll?

Add a theatrical twist to the traditional game of Red Light/Green Light by having students imitate robots and rag dolls. To prepare, demonstrate the jerky, stiff movements of a robot and the limp, lifeless movements of a rag doll; then have students practice these movements. Mark off start and finish lines with tape. To play the game, line the children up across the starting line. Have a volunteer Caller stand behind the finish line and face away from the group. Instruct the Caller to randomly say, "rag doll" or "robot." The group responds by moving toward the finish line in the appropriate way. Encourage the Caller to change the command periodically. Continue the game until one child reaches the finish line. He then becomes the Caller for the next round of the game.

Opposite Acts

Use this acting activity to practice opposite words as well as teamwork. Review the meaning of *opposite* with your class and give some examples. Group students into pairs; then designate one person in each pair to be the leader. Call out a word for the leaders to act out. Then instruct the other child in each pair to act out the *opposite* word. For example, if you call out, "happy," the leader should act happy while his partner acts sad. Change roles after a few rounds so that the other partner has an opportunity to be the leader. What a team!

A Circus Salute

Clown around with your little ones as your group role-plays several of the star attractions under the big top. Take your class outside to a paved playing area. Use chalk to draw three large circles on the pavement. Direct the children to stand in one of the circles. Announce that the jugglers are performing in this ring. Pretend to juggle and encourage your little ones to join in. Move the class to the next circle. Announce that lion trainers are performing here. Lead the group in imitating the motions and commands of a lion trainer. Finally move everyone to the last circle. Announce that the tightrope walkers are performing their act here. Show your youngsters how to portray a balancing tightrope walker. After the demonstrations, invite each child to stand in her favorite ring and strut her stuff! This three-ring circus is sure to be the greatest dramatic-play show on earth!

Everyone Has Emotions

Give youngsters an opportunity to express emotions with this hypothetical-situation game. To play the game, have the class say the chant below; then describe a real-life situation—such as "Someone left the gate open and your dog ran away." Encourage each student to reveal how the described situation would make him feel by showing the emotion on his face.

Frightened, angry, happy, sad…
These are emotions that I've had.
Tell me an imagined case;
I'll show my feelings on my face.

Modeling Manners

If your little ones need reminders about polite behavior, cue them with this role-playing activity. Discuss with your group questions such as "How do you ask someone for a glass of milk?" and "How can you help someone whose feelings have been hurt?" Once your students are cued in on good manners, have two volunteers act out a situation that you set up—such as "Timmy has all the blocks. Jamie wants some. What should they do?" If the actors have trouble coming up with a solution, ask the audience for suggestions. Continue until everyone has a chance to show off her good manners. Your little stars are really shining!

Thank you.

You're welcome.

Hat Tricks

Dramatic play is in the hat with this idea. Gather the hats from your dramatic-play center. Show your class one of the hats; then ask a volunteer to name the person who would wear the selected hat. Pass the hat around the circle, encouraging each child to hold the hat and say something that the wearer of the hat might say. For example, if a firefighter's hat was the object of discussion, a child might say, "I use a hose" or "I am a community helper." Continue sharing hats until everyone has a turn to make a statement. Hats off to dramatic play!

Family Follies

Introduce family diversity by having youngsters dramatize different segments of a family's day. Start the activity with a retelling of *The Three Bears*. Help your youngsters identify the roles of the mother, father, and baby bear; then discuss the similarities and differences among your students' family arrangements. After the discussion, have volunteers act out a family situation—such as eating dinner, getting ready for school, or going shopping. Have the audience help the actors decide which role each actor will portray. For more variation, introduce other family members (student volunteers) to the plot as it develops. Little ones are sure to continue these scenarios on their own in the dramatic-play center.

How's The Weather?

Use nature and weather to provide excellent opportunities for acting. Lead your class in pretending to get ready to go outside on a rainy, cold, or windy day. Once "outside" have children pretend to be things in nature—such as a tree in the wind, a snowman in the sun, or a leaf in autumn. If desired, turn this activity into a guessing game. Have a volunteer act out a type of weather (or an object in a certain type of weather); then invite children to guess what the weather is. Your classroom is sure to be flooded with willing actors and actresses.

Pantomiming Magic

Silence is golden in this activity. Explain to your youngsters that pantomime is an ancient art in which actors use only body movements and facial expressions to perform. Relate pantomiming to the song "If You're Happy And You Know It." (Most children have pantomimed being happy in this song.) Have youngsters stand up and pantomime simple actions such as walking, dancing, and balancing. Once students understand the concept, invite them to pantomime the actions from a favorite class tale as you read the story aloud. Ah, the sounds of silence!

MOVEMENT

MOVEMENT

Exercise youngsters' bodies and brains with these mind-pumping, action-oriented ideas.

ideas contributed by Barbara Backer, Carleen Coderre, Carrie Lacher, Linda Ludlow, Vicki Pacchetti, and Dawn Spurck

In The Wild

Got extra time? Got youngsters with extra energy? Invite them to take a walk in the wild with this game. To begin, divide your class into two teams. Establish start and finish lines; then have each team line up behind the start line. To play, explain that the first child in each line will be the Animal; then whisper the same wild animal name to the two children in that position. On a signal, have the Animals assume the role of the named animal as they move toward the finish line. Invite each team to guess the animal being imitated. If a team has difficulty guessing, ask the Animal to act out more movements or give clues to help his team identify the animal. After the animal is identified, direct the Animal to the end of his team's line; then continue the game, giving the next child in each team's line an opportunity to be a different Animal. Youngsters will go wild over this activity!

Prancing Ponies

Saddle up your little ones for some fancy-prancy fun when they perform the actions mentioned in this song. What a pretty, prancy sight!

(sung to the tune of "Apples And Bananas")

We like to [prance, prance, prance].
We are [prancing ponies].
We like to [prance, prance, prance].
We are [prancing ponies].

Repeat the song, each time replacing the underlined words with one of the suggested sets of words. Or fill in your own words to correspond to seasonal or thematic concepts currently being studied.

crawl and *crawling turtles*
fly and *flying birdies*
swim and *swimming fishies*
jump and *jumping froggies*
squirm and *squirming wormies*
strut and *strutting turkeys*
hop and *hopping bunnies*

Wiggle Worm Workout

Here's a fun way to work in some cooperative counting fun while working the wiggles out of your little ones. Seat youngsters in a circle with adequate space for movement between each child. To begin, ask students to imagine they are worms; then invite them to wiggle and squirm like little worms on the ground. Then call your wormy ones to order to teach them this song. As each number in the song is mentioned, tap a different child on the head to signal her to wiggle like a worm. At the end of the song, have each worm return to her start position. Repeat the song, giving each child the opportunity to be a worm. One wiggle, two wiggle…let's work out those wiggles!

Ten Wiggle Worms
(sung to the tune of "Ten Little Indians")

One wiggle, two wiggle, three wiggle wormies.
Four wiggle, five wiggle, six wiggle wormies.
Seven wiggle, eight wiggle, nine wiggle wormies.
Ten wiggle worms on the ground!

Lyrics With Life

Liven up the lyrics of a well-loved children's song with this idea. First engage youngsters in singing the traditional version of "The Itsy-Bitsy Spider." Then ask the children to suggest how they think the song's spider, waterspout, rain, and sun would act if they all were actually living, feeling beings. For instance, youngsters might say that the spider would be tired and a slow mover, that the waterspout would be ticklish and laugh when it was touched, that the rain would be excited and fall fast and loud, and that the sun would be happy and sway back and forth. After students share their ideas, invite volunteers to each assume the role of a different "character" in the song. Encourage each volunteer to act out his interpretation of that character as the class sings the song. Repeat the song, inviting different volunteers to act out parts so that each child has the opportunity to participate in the role-playing. It's a favorite song come to life!

A Picture-Perfect Performance

Draw a dramatic performance out of your youngsters while promoting their knowledge about things that move. To begin, lead students in a discussion about moving things—such as people, animals, and machines—and how they move. Then give each child a sheet of paper on which to illustrate a thing that moves. Ask each child, in turn, to move like the item he illustrated while your class tries to guess its identity. If necessary, give clues to help the children make a correct guess. Then have the child show his illustration to the class. What rave reviews—it was a picture-perfect performance!

At The Ocean

Create an ocean of motion with this follow-the-leader-style game. Before playing, have youngsters discuss ocean-related things that move and how they move. Then have students stand in an area with adequate space for each child to move freely. Ask them to imagine they are at the beach; then teach them this song. After singing the last line, invite a volunteer to demonstrate actions for the moving thing mentioned in the song; then ask the class to imitate her actions. Have a different volunteer model the movements for the song each time it is repeated. Swish! Flip! Splash! It's a sea of activity!

I Would Move Like This
(sung to the tune of "Mary Had A Little Lamb")

I wish I were a(n) [octopus],
[Octopus], [octopus].
I wish I were a(n) [octopus],
Then I would move like this!

Repeat the song, each time replacing the underlined words with one of these words or phrases, or use one of your own: *jellyfish, tiny crab, big blue whale, great white shark, jumping fish, flying gull, crashing wave, floating boat,* or *gust of wind.*

Frozen In Motion

Chill out with youngsters as they practice their categorizing skills in this creative movement activity. To begin, name a category that contains things that move, such as animals, vehicles, toys, or machines. Explain that students will each perform the movements of something from that category while you play a musical selection. When you stop the music, the children will freeze in place. You will then tap each child, in turn, so that she can melt back into motion and name the thing she is imitating. Then name another category and repeat the activity, using different music, if desired. Music…movement…freeze!

Moving Machines

Construct some interest in the way large construction machinery moves with this song. After teaching youngsters the song, encourage them to mime the actions of the machinery mentioned. Hey-ho! Look at it go!

Hey-Ho! Look At It Go
(sung to the tune of "The Farmer In The Dell")

The backhoe scoops the dirt.
The backhoe scoops the dirt.
Hey-ho! Look at it go!
The backhoe scoops the dirt.

Each time the song is repeated, replace the recurring line with one of the following:

The dozer moves the dirt.
The loader dumps the dirt.
The dump truck bumps away.
The cement mixer spins.
The crane moves up and down.

Colorful Capers

A frenzy of frolicking fun will highlight this colorful game! Prepare youngsters for the game by having them stand in a spacious area so that each child has room for freedom of movement. Ask each student to look at—and take note of—the colors in his clothing. To play, sing this song, inviting those youngsters sporting the named color to perform the action mentioned. Then repeat the song, replacing the color name and action with a different color and action. For example, you might use *blue* and *jump up and down* for the second round of the song, then *yellow* and *fly all around*. Continue the game as long as student interest or time dictates. What colorful fun!

(sung to the tune of "The Wheels On The Bus")

If you're wearing red, spin 'round and 'round,
'Round and 'round,
'Round and 'round.
If you're wearing red, spin 'round and 'round.
Then everyone sit down.

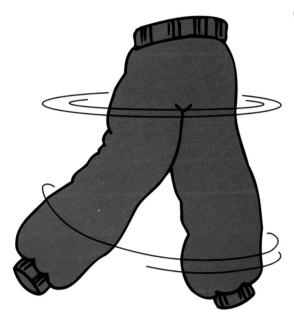

All On A Winter's Day

Do cold winter days put the chill on outdoor play for your class? Then invite indoor movement with this rhyme and a bit of imagination! As you say the rhyme, ask youngsters to act out the roles of the raindrops.

Big and little raindrops falling down with ease.
The winter wind blows. The raindrops freeze.

Cold and frozen raindrops, sparkling in the sun.
Melting, melting, melting…Oh, what fun!

Get In Shape

Youngsters will make a cooperative effort to get in shape with this exercise. Use sidewalk chalk to draw a repeating path of large shapes—such as circles, squares, triangles, rectangles, diamonds, and ovals—on a sidewalk or paved surface. Then invite youngsters to stand at random all around the path. To play, call out a command, such as "Hop to a square." Encourage youngsters to perform the named action as they move to one of the named shapes. As students move about, they will find that two or more children must share the space in a shape so that everyone is in a correct shape. After the first round of play, have students disperse throughout the playing area again; then repeat the procedure, using a different shape name and action. If desired, invite volunteers to take turns naming shapes and actions. Getting in shape together—that's the name of the game!

Moved By Emotions

Help youngsters put their emotions into motion with this familiar tune. Teach students the song; then each time you repeat the song, replace the underlined word with a word to represent a different emotion. At the end of each verse, encourage youngsters to each perform an action to express the mentioned emotion. As you lead the song, you might set its mood and tempo to match the corresponding emotion.

I Can Move Like This
(sung to the tune of "Ten Little Indians")

When I feel [happy], I can move like this.
When I feel [happy], I can move like this.
When I feel [happy], I can move like this.
See how I show I'm [happy]!

What's The Speed Limit?

Youngsters will fine-tune their speedometers when they make speed adjustments during this activity. While you sing this song, encourage children to move as the words suggest. Then repeat the song, replacing the boldface words with a different number (if needed) and body part, such as *two shoulders, two feet,* or *one head.* Continue until time runs out—or until youngsters run out of gas!

(sung to the tune of "Here We Go 'Round The Mulberry Bush")

I have **two arms** that move so slow,
Move so slow, move so slow.
I have **two arms** that move so slow.
Two arms that move so slow!

I have **two arms** that move so fast,
Move so fast, move so fast.
I have **two arms** that move so fast.
Two arms that move so fast!

Gotta Move!

Youngsters need to get up and move? Let 'em show what they know about movement as they perform the words in this bouncy tune.

(sung to the tune of "We Wish You A Merry Christmas")

I know how to [spin] around.
I know how to [spin] around.
I know how to [spin] around.
And safely touch down!

Each time you repeat the song, replace the underlined word with one of the following: *fly, roll, skip, march, bounce, race, sneak,* or *dance.*

SONGS, FINGERPLAYS, AND POEMS

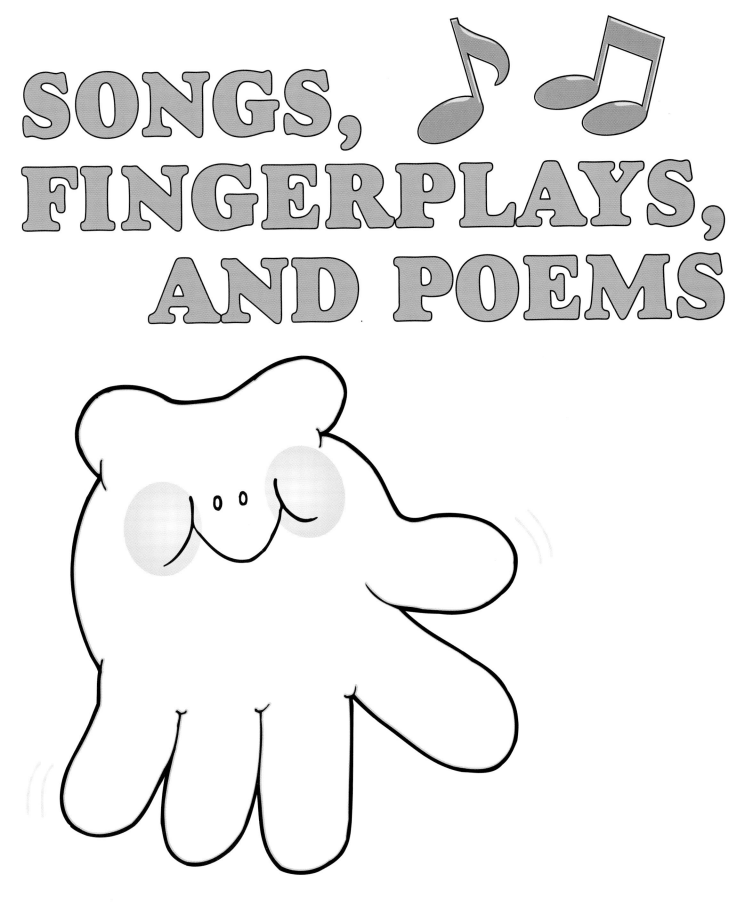

SONGS, FINGERPLAYS, AND POEMS

It doesn't take even a pinch of preparation to teach your youngsters a poem, a song, or a fingerplay from the pages that follow. Focus on important concepts like shapes, colors, numbers, and body parts—or just enjoy some rhythm and rhyme to pass the time!

ideas contributed by Barbara Backer, Rachel Castro, Mary Kathryn Martell, Joyce Montag, Suzanne Moore, Dawn Spurck, and Virginia Zeletzki

Birthday Chant

This chant and activity will help youngsters learn their birth months. After reciting the chant together, call out the months of the year—one at a time. Have each student respond by calling out her name when she hears her birth month.

January, February, March, April, May.
When is your birthday? Is it today?

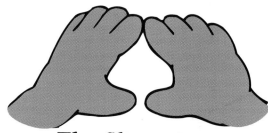

The Shape Rap

Teach little ones this fun rap about making shapes. Encourage them to follow the directions in the rap to make each shape. When you reach the last verse, challenge student pairs to think of as many ways as possible to make squares.

1, 2, 3, 4, 5…
Let's make some shapes come alive!
6, 7, 8, 9, 10…
Let's do it once, then do it again!

Don't get yourself all in a tangle,
Use your fingers to make a triangle!
Finger to finger and thumb to thumb;
Triangle, triangle, here we come!

Shapes are easy as can be.
To make this shape, just follow me!
Make your arms go up and around;
A circle is the shape you've found!

There are lots of ways to make a shape;
With markers, play dough, even tape!
Find a friend and if you dare—
Use your bodies to make a square!

What Color Are You Wearing?

Singing about shoes and shirts? Sure! Help youngsters practice identifying colors with this song. Begin by having your youngsters stand in a circle. Then designate one child to stand in the center. Sing the first line of the song, inserting a solid-colored article of clothing being worn by the child in the center of the circle. Encourage the children to join in. After the child in the center identifies the color, have the class sing the second verse of the song.

(sung to the tune of "The Farmer In The Dell")

What color is your shirt?
What color is your shirt?
Heigh-ho, the derry-o,
What color is your shirt?

Adam's shirt is green.
Adam's shirt is green,
Heigh-ho, the derry-o,
Adam's shirt is green,

After the second verse, have the child standing in the center choose a classmate and switch places with her. Select an article of her clothing and begin the song again.

Touching Colors

This song activity combines practice with colors and body parts. Choose a child to begin the activity. Ask her to name any color and to find something in your classroom that is that color. Encourage her to touch the item she finds with one of her body parts (a finger, an elbow, a knee, etc.). Have the class sing the first verse, inserting the correct name, color, and body part. Then have the children sing the second verse as they search for an item of the same color and touch it with the same body part as the leader. At the end of the second verse, invite the leader to choose a new leader who names a new color. Then continue the activity.

(sung to the tune of "Merrily We Roll Along")

[Jayne] is touching something [red],
Something [red], something [red].
[Jayne] is touching something [red].
She's touching it with her [elbow].

Look around for something [red],
Something [red], something [red].
Look around for something [red],
And touch it the same way.

Get The Wiggles

Teach little ones this movement poem to help them identify body parts. Before you begin, remind them of the names for each part, especially ankles, hips, and elbows.

Wiggle my fingers.	*(Hold up hands and wiggle fingers.)*
Wiggle my toes.	*(Wiggle toes inside shoes.)*
Shrug my shoulders.	*(Shrug shoulders.)*
Touch my nose.	*(Touch nose with one finger.)*
Touch my ankles.	*(Bend down and touch ankles.)*
Touch my hips.	*(Put hands on hips.)*
Bend my knees	
and dip, dip, dip!	*(Bend knees and squat three times.)*
Circle my elbows.	*(Bend arms and circle elbows.)*
Wiggle my ears.	*(Use fingers to wiggle ears.)*
Make my fingers	
disappear!	*(Hide fingers inside fists.)*
Wiggle my eyebrows.	*(Raise and lower eyebrows.)*
Wiggle my knees.	*(Tap knees together.)*
Now I wiggle all of me!	*(Wiggle entire body.)*

The Body-Part Band

Tune up youngsters' awareness of body parts with this song and its accompanying movements.

(sung to the tune of "The Farmer In The Dell")

I use my body parts. I use my body parts.
I think I am so smart to use my body parts.

I use my little hand to lead my little band.
    (Wave hand like conductor.)
I think I am so smart to use this body part.

I use my little thumbs to play my little drums.
    (Use thumbs like drumsticks.)
I think I am so smart to use this body part.

I use my elbow bone to slide my big trombone.
    (Pretend to play trombone.)
I think I am so smart to use this body part.

My fingers play the keys of the piano on my knees.
    (Wiggle fingers on knees.)
I think I am so smart to use this body part.

I use my little wrist; my tambourine I twist.
    (Pretend to shake tambourine.)
I think I am so smart to use this body part.

I'm finished with my song. That didn't take too long.
I think I am so smart to use my body parts!

Where Are The Numbers?

This song will help little ones practice number recognition *and* explore feelings. If desired use a washable marker to write the numerals 1–5 on the fingertips of one of your hands before you perform the song.

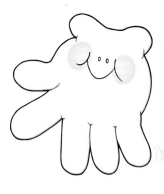

(sung to the tune of "Where Is Thumbkin?")

Where is One? Where is One?
Here I am. Here I am.
    (Hold up one finger.)
How are you today, One?
Happy—having lots of fun!
    (Make finger "dance.")
Who is next? Who is next?

Where is Two? Where is Two?
Here I am. Here I am.
    (Hold up two fingers.)
How are you today, Two?
Sad and feeling kind of blue.
    (Make a sad face.)
Who is next? Who is next?

Where is Three? Where is Three?
Here I am. Here I am.
    (Hold up three fingers.)
How are you today, Three?
Sleepy, sleepy as can be.
    (Yawn.)
Who is next? Who is next?

Where is Four? Where is Four?
Here I am. Here I am.
    (Hold up four fingers.)
How are you today, Four?
Hungry as a dinosaur!
    (Rub tummy.)
Who is next? Who is next?

Where is Five? Where is Five?
Here I am. Here I am.
    (Hold up five fingers.)
How are you today, Five?
Excited just to be alive!
    (Wiggle all fingers.)
Now we're done.
That was fun!
    (Clap.)

When I Say...

Get the attention of restless little ones with this action poem. After saying the poem together many times, try calling out a number between one and ten. Can your students remember the accompanying action for each number? They'll certainly have fun trying!

When I say, "one," put up your thumb.
When I say, "two," put a hand on your shoe.
When I say, "three," put a hand on your knee.
When I say, "four," fall on the floor.
When I say, "five," let's go for a drive.
When I say, "six," play your finger sticks.
When I say, "seven," jump up to heaven.
When I say, "eight," open the gate.
When I say, "nine," put a hand on your spine.
When I say, "ten," sit down again.

Hands Up High

Try this action poem to transition your youngsters from high-energy activities to quieter class times.

Hands up high! Hands down low!
Hands reach down to touch your toes!
(Reach down and touch toes.)

Hands up high! Hands down low!
Hands reach up to grow, grow, GROW!
(Stretch both hands toward ceiling.)

Hands up high! Hands down low!
Hands in front and say, "Hello!"
(Wave both hands in front of body.)

Hands up high! Hands down low!
Hands to the side and row, row, row your boat....
(Make rowing motions and begin singing.)

Hands up high! Hands down low!
Hands on hips and tippy-toe.
(Place hands on hips, tiptoe to your seat, and sit down.)

Hands up high! Hands down low!
Hands in laps just like so!
(Place hands in lap.)

In The Driver's Seat

Your youngsters will enjoy driving pretend pickup trucks all over your classroom as you recite this rhyme together several times. Each time you come to the blank in line five, ask a different child to choose an item she'd like to load into the back of her imaginary truck. Stop the rhyme as your little ones dramatize the loading of their trucks with the named item. Then have them all jump into their driver's seats and continue the ride!

I can drive my truck
All around the town,
Driving up the hills
And then back down.
I fill my truck with _____.
I jump inside and then...
I drive around the town until
I come back home again.

pumpkins

Color-Mixing Song

Review how colors are made with this tune. As an extension, provide the materials for children to use to explore color mixing—such as colored water, watercolor paints, colored chalk, or colored cellophane scraps.

*(sung to the tune of
"Miss Lucy Had A Baby")*

Red and blue make purple;
Blue and yellow make green;
Yellow and red make orange—
The best I've ever seen!
Red and green make brown;
But how do we get black?
Just put them all together,
And you're on the right track!

The Animals On The Farm

Focusing on farm animals? After reviewing facts that children have learned about critters on the farm, teach your youngsters this tune. Make up your own verses to sing about any animal's sound or other characteristics.

(sung to the tune of "Dem Bones")

The cow on the farm goes moo, moo.
The cow on the farm goes moo, moo.
The cow on the farm goes moo, moo.
Moo, moo, moo, moo, moo.

The cow's long tail goes swish, swish.
The cow's long tail goes swish, swish.
The cow's long tail goes swish, swish.
Swish, swish, swish, swish, swish.

The cow makes milk for me to drink.
The cow makes milk for me to drink.
The cow makes milk for me to drink.
Drink, drink, drink, drink, drink.

Five Little Friends

Invite your little actors and actresses to dramatize this counting poem about a very familiar situation—going to school! Ask five volunteers to act out the poem as you and the other youngsters recite it. Then repeat the poem with new groups of volunteers until everyone has had a turn to act. (Replace the word "preschool" with "kindergarten" if it is more appropriate for your age group.)

Five little friends playing on the floor;
One went to preschool, and then
    there were four.

Four little friends playing by a tree;
One went to preschool, and then
    there were three.

Three little friends—a happy crew;
One went to preschool, and then
    there were two.

Two little friends having lots of fun;
One went to preschool, and then
    there was one.

One little friend looking for someone;
He (she) went to preschool, and then
    there were none.

Come with us to preschool and
    when you arrive,
You'll meet some new friends—1, 2, 3, 4, 5!

GAMES

GAMES

Gather your little ones together and play a game or two. These require little or no preparation, so you can be ready for some fun—and learning—at a moment's notice!

ideas contributed by Rachel Castro, Linda Gordetsky, Ellen Weiss, and Virginia Zeletzki

Loud And Clear

Youngsters can exercise their auditory discrimination skills with this game. Choose one child to be the Mouse and one child to be your helper. Seat the Mouse in a chair and blindfold him. Ask the class to recite the following poem:

> There was a little mouse
> Sitting in his little house.
> A sound came loud and clear.
> What was it, Mousey dear?

At the end of the rhyme, have your helper use a common object in the room to make a familiar sound. For example, your helper might run the water in the sink, open and close a closet door, or shake a tambourine. Once the Mouse identifies the sound, he becomes your helper for the next round and a new Mouse is chosen.

Funny Voices

Further sharpen children's auditory discrimination skills with this activity. Have one child (the Guesser) step away from the group while you choose a child to be the Counter. Once the Guesser has returned to the group, blindfold her or cover her eyes with your hands. Have the Counter use a funny, disguised voice to count from one to ten. Give the Guesser three chances to identify the Counter. If she is successful, allow her to choose the Counter for the next round. Give the former Counter a turn to be the Guesser, and continue the game until every child has had a turn to guess.

Where Are My Kittens?

Little ones will be all ears when you play this game! Designate one child as the Cat. Have the Cat step away from the group while you choose six children to be Kittens. (You may want to place a sticker on the palm of each Kitten's hand to remind him of his role.) Instruct the Kittens to begin meowing. Have all the children (including the Kittens) hold their hands in front of their mouths. Then invite the Cat to rejoin the group and listen carefully to distinguish which children are the six Kittens. Remind the Kittens to continue meowing until the Cat finds all of them. Once all the Kittens are found, choose a new Cat and Kittens and begin again.

Vary this game by asking children to play the roles of other familiar animal mothers and babies—such as Dog and Puppies, Sheep and Lambs, or Hen and Chicks.

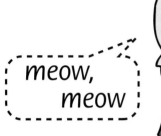

My Grandma's Soup

Try this variation of a traditional game to test students' auditory memories. Seat youngsters in a circle and teach them the following rhyme:

I had the croup, and my grandma made me soup.
Since I was so sick, she made it extra thick!
Into the pot went _____ .

Designate one child to begin the game by naming a food to fill in the blank. Then repeat the rhyme and have the next child in the circle repeat the food named by the first child and add another to the list. Continue around the circle with each child attempting to name all the previous foods and adding one of her own. When the list becomes too lengthy for a child to remember, start the game over.

Mary's Little Lambs

Youngsters won't be sheepish about playing this game! Have the children stand in a circle with their arms raised and their hands joined, forming arches. Designate one child to be Mary (or Manny). As youngsters sing the first two verses of "Mary Had A Little Lamb," have Mary go in and out of the circle, passing beneath the children's arms. When the children begin the second verse ("And everywhere that Mary went..."), have Mary tap the child closest to her. That child becomes her Lamb and begins following her in and out of the circle. (Instruct the rest of the children to close up the circle.) At the end of the second verse, have the Lamb tap the child closest to him, who then becomes a Lamb, too. Both Lambs follow Mary as the children sing the variation.

Traditional

Mary had a little lamb,
Little lamb, little lamb.
Mary had a little lamb,
Its fleece was white as snow.

And everywhere that Mary went,
Mary went, Mary went,
Everywhere that Mary went,
That lamb was sure to go.

Variation

Mary had [two] little lambs,
Little lambs, little lambs.
Mary had [two] little lambs,
With fleece as white as snow.

And everywhere that Mary went,
Mary went, Mary went,
Everywhere that Mary went,
Those lambs were sure to go.

Have children continue to repeat the variation, substituting the words *three, four, five,* etc., for the underlined word. As more Lambs are added and the circle grows smaller, it will become increasingly difficult for the line of Lambs to weave in and out without bumping into one another. End the game with your giggling youngsters by substituting new words for the final line: "Those lambs just couldn't go!"

Duck, Duck, Goose Revisited

Tired of Duck, Duck, Goose, but the children aren't? Try some variations. Play the game as you normally would, but substitute other words that tie into your current theme—maybe "Pumpkin, Pumpkin, Jack-O'-Lantern" or "Bunny, Bunny, Carrot."

For more of a challenge, take the part of the Picker yourself, walking around the outside of the circle of seated students, tapping children on their heads as you go. Name items that belong to a particular category. When you reach the child you want to choose, say a word that doesn't fit the category. The chosen child should jump up and chase you once around the circle, trying to tag you before you reach his seat. If the child manages to tag you, allow him to choose the next category by whispering it into your ear. Once more advanced students have the idea, give each of them an opportunity to be the Picker.

Animal Freeze Tag

Try a fun twist on the traditional game of Freeze Tag. Choose an animal and instruct all the players—including It—to move like that animal while playing the game. For example, have all the players move like penguins, with their legs and heels together, waddling from side to side. Or ask youngsters to hop like kangaroos, gallop like horses, or slither like snakes.

Cat, Mouse, And Dog

If your children like the traditional game of Cat and Mouse, introduce them to this fun variation. Have the children form a circle and hold hands. Designate one child to be the Mouse, one child to be the Cat, and one child to be the Dog. Have the Mouse stand inside the circle and instruct the Cat and Dog to stand outside the circle. As in the traditional game, the Cat tries to catch (tag) the Mouse. The Mouse and Cat can go in and out of the circle by ducking under children's arms. The children forming the circle can raise or lower their arms to block the Cat or allow the Mouse to get away. However, the Dog must remain outside the circle. His job is to try to catch the Cat. When either the Mouse or the Cat is caught, replace all three players with different children and begin again.

Off The Wall

This relay race is perfect to play in a gymnasium. Divide your class into two or more teams and provide each team with a playground ball. Have each team line up with one child behind another. To begin, the first child in line passes the ball overhead to the child behind him. The team members pass the ball overhead to the end of the line. The last child takes the ball, runs to a designated wall, and bounces the ball off the wall. He then catches (or chases) the ball, then runs with it to the front of his team's line to begin passing it overhead again. The first team to have all children bounce the ball off the wall and all team members back in their original lineup is the winner.

Jack And Jill

How about some nursery-rhyme racing? Divide your class into boys and girls and have the two groups line up facing one another, about two yards apart. Make chalk or tape lines to delineate the two ends of the alley formed between the lines of children. Beginning at one end of this alley, have a boy and a girl—Jack and Jill—stand behind the starting line and skip together to the opposite end of the space as the class sings the traditional song "Jack And Jill." When Jack and Jill arrive at the other end of the alley and the children reach the part of the song where "Jack fell down," Jack and Jill turn and race back to the starting line. They then join their respective lines at the far end and the boy and girl closest to the starting line become Jack and Jill, skipping to one end and racing back. The game ends when everyone has raced. If desired, keep score and give each team one point for each race won.

Up In The Air

Use a lightweight ball, such as a beach ball, or a balloon to play this cooperative game. The object of the game is to keep the ball in the air, not letting it touch the ground for as long as possible. Explain to students that when the ball comes to them, they should either catch it and throw it up into the air again or tap it up volleyball-fashion. Have the children count aloud with you the number of times the ball is tapped up or caught and thrown. The game ends when the ball hits the ground. Encourage students to try to better their score on the next round of play.

Monkeying Around With Mr. Alligator

Are your little ones familiar with the counting rhyme about the monkeys who tease the alligator? Then they'll love this game! Use a sidewalk crack or create a chalk or tape line on the floor or on a concrete play area to represent a river. Mark the two ends of the line to clearly delineate the playing area. Designate one child to be the Alligator and another child to be the Monkey Leader. The Monkey Leader stands on one side of the river, and all the other children (the Monkeys) stand on the opposite side. The Alligator must stay on the line, but can run along it from end to end.

To play, the Monkey Leader calls the Monkeys to cross the river. All the Monkeys try to run past the Alligator without being tagged. All the Monkeys who are tagged must sit in a designated spot (the Alligator's lair). Then the Monkey Leader goes to the opposite side and calls the untagged Monkeys to cross the river again, this time running in the opposite direction. When only two children are left untagged, they become the Alligator and the Monkey Leader for the next round of play.

Wastebasket Ball

Here's an activity that combines critical thinking and eye-hand coordination. Divide your class into three or four groups. Have each group line up—one child behind another—with the first child in each line an equal distance from a large wastebasket. Assign a color to each team. Give each child a small piece of paper that corresponds to her team's color. To play the game, give a clue about one of the team's colors, such as "It's the color of grass." The child at the front of the green team's line then wads up his paper and throws it, attempting to get it into the wastebasket. That child then goes to the end of his team's line. Continue giving clues about the colors until every child has had a chance to shoot. Then count the number of each color of paper wad in the basket. The team who made the most baskets wins!

Tick-Tock-Go!

This game for 13 players will help youngsters memorize the arrangement of the numbers on a clock face. Arrange 12 children in a circle, positioning them to imitate the placement of the numbers on a clock (with 12 across from 6, etc.). Have the children sit down once they're in position. Use chalk to write the numeral in front of each child, or write it on a piece of masking tape and stick it to the floor or carpet. Have another child sit in the center of the circle. Then have the children recite this rhyme:

> One, two, three, four, five, six, seven...
> Eight, nine, ten, and then eleven.
> Twelve is at the top, you know;
> Time for a game of **Tick-Tock-*Go!***

After the rhyme is recited, the child in the center of the circle calls out two numbers on the clock face. The children sitting in those two spots must jump up and run to switch places. The child sitting in the center attempts to take one of their places while they are switching. The child who loses her seat then sits in the center for the next round of play.

Materials
At Your Fingertips

Quick! Bring on the beanbags, turn to the teddy-bear counters, and pass the paper plates! There are dozens of on-the-spot activities you can do with the materials and manipulatives you have on hand in your early-childhood classroom. Just turn the pages that follow for some great suggestions!

Instant Activities With...
Craft Sticks

ideas contributed by Barbara Backer, Angie Kutzer, and Vicki Pacchetti

Have each child glue two sticks together to resemble an airplane. After the glue dries, invite her to "fly" her aircraft while singing the following song to the tune of "Mary Had A Little Lamb":

See my airplane fly around,
In the air, off the ground.
Flying low, then flying high,
Way up in the sky.

Ask each child to draw, color, and cut out pictures of his favorite story's characters. Have him tape or glue each character to a different craft stick to make stick puppets. Encourage small groups to use the puppets to dramatize stories.

Try this open-ended art activity. Encourage each student to make a picture with her craft sticks by arranging sticks on her paper, gluing them in place, and using crayons to add any missing details. Display the finished stick pics on a bulletin board.

Divide your class into pairs and provide each pair with several craft sticks. Call out the name of a shape. Have student pairs arrange their craft sticks into the designated shape. Extend the activity by calling out letters and numerals and asking youngsters to perform more stick tricks.

Two craft sticks really keep the beat! Give each child a pair of sticks. Have him listen, then repeat a pattern that you tap. Call out a number and challenge him to tap his sticks the appropriate number of times. And the beat goes on!

Have each child decorate one side of two craft sticks with a matching pattern. Divide the children into small groups and invite each group to play a quick memory game. Direct each group to combine its sticks and lay them out, facedown. Then have youngsters take turns turning over sticks attempting to find matching pairs.

Use craft sticks for measuring activities. Direct each student to place her sticks end-to-end to measure the length of a classmate's body, a tabletop, or a big book. Challenge her to find an object in the room that is two sticks long. For added fun, take the craft sticks outdoors with your class and measure a seesaw, slide, or sandbox.

Act out the traditional song "Ten In A Bed" with craft-stick figures. Give each child ten craft sticks and an 8" x 10" sheet of construction paper. Have him use a marker to draw a face at the top of each stick. To make the bed, fold the construction paper lengthwise as shown; then staple or tape the sides. Direct the child to put the sticks into the bed; then start singing. Roll over, roll over!

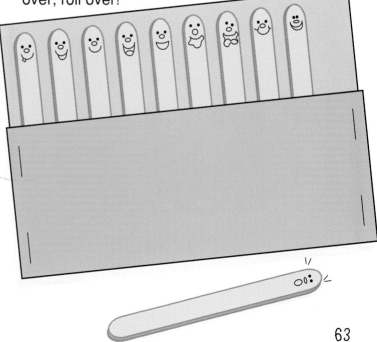

Encourage imaginations with this sweet idea. Have each child use colored-paper scraps and glue to make her own lollipop, then glue it to a craft stick. Ask each child to dictate a short story about her unique confection. Invite her to share her story and lollipop with the rest of the class.

Gather together a handful of craft sticks. Mark one of the sticks with a star. Insert the sticks into an envelope, a bag, a can, or another handy container. Pass the container around a circle of seated children. Instruct each child to pull out a stick. If he pulls out a plain stick, he puts it back and passes the container to the next person. If he draws the star stick, he performs a short act for the group—such as reciting a nursery rhyme, saying the alphabet, or singing a favorite song—before returning the stick and passing the container.

Give each child a craft stick and head out to the sandbox. Instruct each student to dig a hole using only the stick. Whose hole is the biggest?

Help your youngsters create and solve their own craft-stick puzzles. For each child, tape eight craft sticks together, side by side as shown. Have the child use crayons or markers to draw a picture, covering all of the sticks. Then remove the tape, mix up the sticks, and challenge the child to put her puzzle back together or to create another interesting design. For more advanced children, have them draw a letter, shape, or numeral on their stick puzzles for a classmate to solve.

Play some lively classical tunes and invite your children to be the guest conductors. Give each child a craft-stick baton to keep the beat and lead the orchestra. Move over Leonard Bernstein!

Divide your class into pairs. Give each pair five craft sticks; then instruct the pair to place the sticks on the floor or tabletop between them. To play this critical-thinking game, one partner closes his eyes while the other partner takes sticks from the middle and hides them behind her back. The first child then opens his eyes and guesses how many sticks his partner took. The partner reveals the sticks to check the guess. Have the children take turns hiding the sticks until interest wanes.

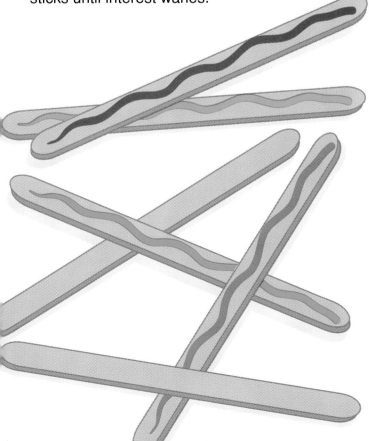

Give each small group or pair of students a handful of craft sticks. Have children use markers or crayons to decorate one side of each stick. To play this counting and comparing game, each child takes a turn picking up the sticks, then dropping them onto a tabletop. The child may keep the sticks that land with the decorated sides showing. Play continues until no sticks are left. Have the children count their sticks to see who collected the most. Ready for another round?

The key word is *balance* in this activity. Give each child a craft stick. Direct him to experiment with balancing the stick on as many body parts as possible. Make a list of all the discoveries that are made.

Instant Activities With...

POM-POMS

ideas contributed by Joyce Montag

Scatter pom-poms on the floor of your classroom. Divide your class into groups so that there is one group for each color of pom-pom. Assign one color to each group and instruct each group to gather all the pom-poms of its designated color. Have each group work together to count the total number of pom-poms they collect. Then make a simple graph on the chalkboard or a sheet of chart paper to show the results.

Give each child one pom-pom. Ask him to attempt to balance the pom-pom on various designated body parts, such as his arm, shoulder, head, or finger, or on the back of his hand. For an added challenge, ask each child to walk around the room while balancing a pom-pom on a particular body part.

Scatter a large number of pom-poms around your classroom. Then provide each child with a 12-inch piece of clear or masking tape. Direct children to collect as many pom-poms as they can, using only the sticky side of their tape pieces to touch the pompoms. When everyone has finished his collection, have each child count to determine how many pompoms are stuck to his tape.

Have each child choose a partner, and give one child in each pair a pompom. Have the partners sit on the carpet facing one another. Give commands using positional words, such as "Place the pom-pom *next to* your partner's leg," or "Put the pom-pom *behind* your partner." After you've given several commands, have the partners switch roles, and continue the activity with new commands.

A playground parachute is ideal to use with this activity, but any large piece of cloth will also work. Look around your classroom for an old sheet, a blanket from your housekeeping area, or even a drop cloth. Depending on the size of the cloth, have either a large or a small group of children hold the edges of the cloth so that it is taut. Place an assortment of pom-poms in the center of the cloth. Then instruct the children to shake the cloth to make waves of increasing intensity as they chant the following rhyme. Tell youngsters that when they reach the end of the rhyme, they can make the pom-poms "explode" all over the room. They'll be more than willing to help you clean up so they can try this activity again!

Pour the corn into the pot.
Pop-Pop-Pop!
Shake it, shake it 'til it's hot.
Pop-Pop-Pop!
Lift the lid; what have we got?
Pop-Pop-Pop-Pop-POPCORN!

 Gather several sheets of paper and label each one with a numeral from 1 to 12 (or other numerals appropriate for your age group). Lay the papers in numerical order on the floor. Use chalk or a piece of masking tape to make a line parallel to and about three feet from the line of papers. Then have each child choose a partner, and give one child in each pair a pom-pom. Working with one pair of students at a time, have one partner identify a numeral on the floor. Instruct the other partner to stand behind the chalk or tape line and try to toss the pair's pom-pom onto that numeral. Then have the partners switch roles. Continue until all the pairs have had a turn.

 Distribute a pom-pom to each child. Have her cup her hands together and toss the pom-pom into the air, then catch it. Have each child count how many times she can successfully throw and catch her pom-pom.

 Invite youngsters to create some pretty pom-pom jewelry! Give each child a sheet of paper, a pair of scissors, a few pom-poms, glue, and some tape. Show the children how to cut the paper into very short strips to make rings, longer strips to make bracelets, and any shape to make a pin. Then invite the children to glue pom-poms to the paper strips and shapes (or to attach them with rolled pieces of tape). Oh, what colorful gemstones!

Instant Activities With...
Rhythm Instruments

ideas contributed by Rachel Castro and Carrie Lacher

Have the children sit in a circle. Provide a set of bells or shakers for each child. Invite the children to shake their instruments for a minute or two; then ask them to stop. Encourage them to start and stop shaking their instruments on your command several times. Then teach them this rhyme. Say the rhyme together a few times, having them stop and start shaking their instruments as indicated.

Tiny mouse, tiny mouse, time for bed.
Shhhh!   (Stop shaking instruments.)
Tiny mouse, tiny mouse, raise your head.
Wake up!   (Shake instruments.)

Tune into patterns with a listening activity. Gather several instruments. Play the instruments in turn to create a pattern, such as *drum, triangle, drum, triangle.* Then invite a volunteer to play the same instruments, copying your pattern.

Gather a few different instruments. Remind the children of the name for each instrument; then play each one as youngsters listen. Then have one child at a time sit with her back to the group as you play one of the instruments. Ask the child to identify the instrument she hears.

Give each child a set of rhythm sticks. Then teach the class the following rhyme to help them practice the concept of opposites. Explain that when they reach the line that says "Tap all alone," you will choose one child (by touching her shoulder) to tap alone. Then everyone can join in on the last line.

Tap up high.
Tap down low.
Tap really fast.
Tap really slow.
Tap really soft.
Tap really loud.
Tap all alone.
Tap in a crowd.

68

Invite youngsters to play along with this lively tune. Pass out drums, rhythm sticks, and triangles to your youngsters. If you don't have enough for everyone, sing the song several times until everyone has had a turn to play an instrument.

(sung to the tune of "This Old Man")

Put your drum on your knee.
Play that drum now just for me.
With a rat, tat, tatty-tat,
Tummy-tum-tum,
Music time is so much fun!

Got your sticks? Yessiree!
Tap your sticks now just for me.
With a tap, tap, tappy-tap,
Tappy-tap-tum,
Music time is so much fun!

Is that a triangle that I see?
Play your triangle just for me.
With a ding, ding, ding-a-ling,
Ring-a-ring-rung.
Music time is so much fun!

Give each child a set of rhythm sticks. Write a numeral on the chalkboard (or on a large sheet of paper). Ask a volunteer to tap his sticks together for the corresponding number of beats. Continue with other numerals until every child in the group has had a turn.

Place a drum, a set of sticks, a bell, and a set of blocks in front of the group. Review the name of each instrument. Then say a word that rhymes with the name of one of the instruments, such as "shell." Ask for a volunteer to play the instrument that rhymes with your word.

Choose several instruments that have distinct shapes. For example, you might choose a tambourine, a set of blocks, and a triangle. Show each of the instruments to the group and discuss the shape of each instrument. Then say to one child, "Play the [circle]." Invite her to find the instrument with the corresponding shape and play it for the group. To make the activity more challenging, ask the child to play the instruments in a series, such as "Play the circle, then the rectangles, then the triangle."

69

Instant Activities With...

STRAWS

ideas contributed by Ada Goren and Vicki Pacchetti

Show your little ones how to join straws to-gether by pinching the end of one straw and inserting it into the end of another straw. Once they've mastered this, invite them to create straw shapes. Encourage each child to push three or four straws together into a long length and then bend the straws to form various shapes, such as a triangle, a square, or a rectangle. (Little ones may have more success if you reinforce each seam with a piece of clear tape.)

Let your young artists' imaginations run wild as they create straw sculptures. Give each youngster a handful of straws, and invite him to join and bend the straws as he desires to create an original design. Or—if your straw supply is limited—have children work in pairs to create straw sculptures.

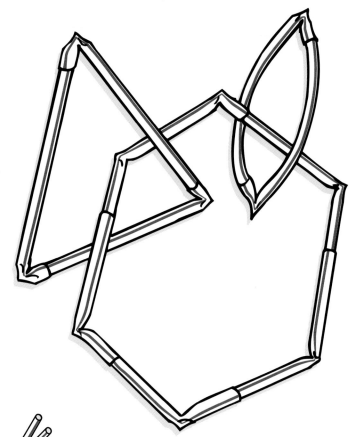

Get your little ones moving and grooving! Give each child a straw and ask her to hold one end of the straw in each hand. Tell the chil-dren to apply some "invisible glue" to their fingers to lock the straws into place. Then encourage the chil-dren to stretch and move in different, wiggly ways without ever letting their fingers leave the straws.

On your mark, get set,…let's have a race! Divide your class into groups of four or five students. Give each child in the first group a dif-ferent color of paper to wad into a ball. Also give each child her own straw. Then mark start and fin-ish lines on the floor with masking tape. Have each child in the group kneel behind the start line and place her paper ball on the line. Then chal-lenge the children to move their balls to the finish line by blowing through their straws. Repeat the race with the other groups of children, using the same paper balls and fresh straws each time.

You've heard of pick-up sticks? Why not pick-up straws? Divide your class into pairs of children and give one child in each pair a handful of straws. Demonstrate how to hold the straws vertically in one hand about three inches off the floor. Then have each pair drop their straws and play a game similar to pick-up sticks. Each player takes a turn trying to pick up a straw without nudging any of the others. If the player is successful, he may pick up another straw. If he is unsuccessful, play moves to his partner. The object of this game is to pick up the final straw.

Demonstrate how to join straws together by pinching one end of a straw and inserting it into the end of another straw. Ask each child to join together three straws in this fashion. Then give each child a small piece of colored paper, and ask her to write her name on the paper and decorate it as she desires. Assist each child in taping her name paper to the end of her supersized straw. Voilà! Each child has a personalized pointer!

Adam likes to sip strawberry milkshakes through a straw.

Give each child two or three straws and a pair of scissors. Instruct him to cut the straws into various lengths. Then ask him to place the straw pieces in order from longest to shortest or from shortest to longest.

Straws are for sipping! What do your little ones like to drink through a straw? Have each child draw a picture of his favorite beverage. Then help him cut a small slit in the top of his drawing and insert a real straw into the slit to complete the picture. Tape the straw into place on the back of the drawing. If time allows, write "[Child's name] likes to sip [beverage] through a straw," on each child's paper.

Instant Activities With...
HOOPS

ideas contributed by Diane Gilliam

O Use a hoop to stimulate some self-esteem. Have one child at a time stand in front of the group, holding a hoop in front of him. Ask the class to recite the rhyme below; then have the child behind the hoop (or Magic Mirror) tell one reason he is special. Continue until every child has had a turn.

Magic Mirror, whom do you see?
We see [Child's name], as special as can be!

O Place three rows of hoops on the floor to represent a giant tic-tac-toe board. Then divide your class into two teams; designate one team to be the Xs and the other to be the Os. Ask the first child on one team to answer a question to review the skill of your choice (for example, "What's a word that rhymes with *hand?*" or "Name a word that begins with the sound of *T*"). If the child responds correctly, he may choose a hoop and stand inside it. Alternate questions between the teams until one team successfully completes any row going vertically, horizontally, or diagonally.

How about some monster measuring? Begin by reviewing proper measurement techniques, such as a *starting point, spacing,* and *straight lines.* Then divide your class into small groups, and give each group one or two hoops. Assign each group a specific distance to measure on your school playground or along a hallway. Just how many hoops is it between the balance beam and the monkey bars?

O Review the types of foods that belong at each level of the Food Guide Pyramid. Then lay several hoops on the floor to represent the Food Guide Pyramid. Ask youngsters to draw pictures of foods from each section of the pyramid. Then have them place their illustrations in the appropriate hoops.

For some indoor movement fun, provide each child with a hoop. Have each child lay her hoop on the floor and stand beside it. Then teach your little ones the following song *(sung to the tune of "Mary Had A Little Lamb")* and invite them to march around their individual hoops. Fill in a new action word for the underlined word each time you repeat the verse.

See the children [hop] around,
[Hop] around, [hop] around.
See the children [hop] around,
[Hop] around their hoops.

Scatter a class supply of hoops on your playground, and have each child stand inside a hoop. Invite your youngsters to imagine that they are forest animals in the woods. Then call out an action word, such as *skip.* Encourage the children to begin skipping around the playground. Then call out a warning that a hunter or a stranger is nearby. Encourage your little animals to skip to the safety of their hoops. When everyone is back in his hoop, tell youngsters that the coast is clear. Then call out a new action word, such as *gallop, hop,* or *jog.*

Use hoops as personal spaces for dramatic play. Have each child stand inside a hoop as he acts out given scenarios. Try any of the following or come up with more of your own:

- a sprouting seed
- a tree in the wind
- a hatching chick
- a blossoming flower
- a bear waking from hibernation

Instant Activities With...
Paper and Crayons

ideas contributed by Linda Gordetsky, Ada Goren, and Joyce Montag

Have each child choose a partner. Give each pair of students a box of eight crayons (or a collection of the eight basic colors). Have the children lay the eight crayons on the tabletop in front of them. Invite one child to turn her back while the other child removes one of the crayons and holds it in her lap. Ask the first child to turn around and determine which crayon is missing. Then have the partners switch roles.

Encourage cooperation with a class drawing of a snowman. Mount a large piece of bulletin-board paper on the wall at the children's level. Provide a large box of crayons on the floor in front of the paper. Invite your youngsters to line up and—one at a time—contribute to the drawing. Have the first child begin by drawing the large circle for the snowman's bottom. Then have each child in turn add other features, such as the snowman's body, head, nose, eyes, scarf, hat, arms, etc. If desired, encourage the children to write a class story about the finished snowman.

Give each child a sheet of white paper and some crayons. Demonstrate how to draw a scribble design without lifting your crayon from the paper. As lines are crossed again and again, various shapes and spaces will be created. Instruct students to make their own scribble designs, then to color in the spaces with different crayons to create a stained-glass effect. Display the finished designs in your classroom windows.

Cooperate to create an alphabet orchard! For each small group, provide a length of bulletin-board paper and a supply of crayons. (Or, if desired, have each child make a separate drawing on an individual sheet of paper.) Demonstrate how to trace around your hand and forearm to create the shape of a tree trunk and branches. Have each of your little ones trace around his own arm and hand in an open space on the bulletin-board paper. Then invite each student to write letters on the branches of his tree. If children run out of room, invite them to trace new trees and fill the branches with more letters! Display all the papers together on a bulletin board with the title "Our Alphabet Orchard."

Give each child a sheet of paper and some crayons. Demonstrate how to fold the top two corners of the paper so that they meet in the center. Then ask children to add a door and windows to this shape to make it resemble a house. Instruct each student to turn her paper over and draw a picture of her family on the opposite side. Encourage students to share their pictures with the class before taking them home.

Encourage little ones to experiment with the effect of holding two crayons in one hand as they draw a picture. Then have them try three crayons. Invite them to share their original designs with their classmates.

Paper and crayons aren't just for art! Practice counting, graphing, and the concepts of *more, fewer,* and *equal* with a crayon graph. Prepare a simple graph on a sheet of bulletin-board paper. Then provide a large supply of crayons in the basic colors. Encourage the children to sort the crayons by color. Have them help you fill in the class graph by taking turns coloring a square for each crayon counted in each color. Compare the results shown on the graph. Of which color did you have the most crayons? Of which color did you have the fewest? Were there the same number of crayons in any colors?

Have each child draw a picture on a sheet of paper. Then provide each child with a pair of scissors. Ask him to cut his drawing into a few pieces and mix them up. Then challenge him to reconstruct his picture. If youngsters are successful with putting together their own puzzles, invite each of them to switch seats with a friend and try to put together a new puzzle.

Divide your class into small groups. Give each child a sheet of paper and crayons. Invite each child to draw one object on her paper. Instruct the children that they must stop drawing when you give a signal, such as ringing a bell. When you give the signal, have each child pass her paper to the child next to her. Explain that each child should add to the drawing he receives until you give the signal again. Continue passing and drawing until each child in the group has added to each drawing. Then show the pictures one at a time. Have the group make up a story about each picture.

The theme is cooperation with this class artistic endeavor! Begin by drawing a large outline that corresponds with your current theme on a piece of bulletin-board paper (for example, you could outline a heart, a flower, or a dinosaur). Then provide drawing paper and crayons. Ask each child to draw a colorful design on his paper. Then invite him to tear the design into pieces. Have each child bring some or all of his pieces to you to glue onto the large outline. Keep the class design on display throughout your thematic unit.

Ask each youngster to pick a partner. Give each pair some paper and crayons (for younger children, use a selection of basic colors). Have one child, the Guesser, turn away as his partner, the Artist, selects a crayon and draws something on the paper with it. Then have the Artist replace the crayon before the Guesser turns around. Have the Guesser guess which crayon the Artist used to make the drawing. If he desires, the Guesser may draw something next to the original drawing to check his guess. Then have the partners switch roles and play again.

Older children will enjoy reviewing the alphabet with this activity. Make a list of objects for each letter of the alphabet. Ask each child to choose a letter (or more than one letter, depending on the size of your group) and draw the letter and an accompanying object on a sheet of paper. When all the letters have been illustrated, display the papers on a bulletin board to create an alphabet quilt.

Students can both create and play this game of Name Bingo. Give each child a sheet of drawing paper. Demonstrate how to fold the paper in half three times, then open it to reveal eight boxes. Have each child take her unfolded paper—or bingo card—to a classmate and ask him to sign his name in one of the boxes. Have children continue until everyone has a name in every box. Then you're ready to play! Call out the names of your students randomly. Direct each child to look for the name that you call and mark that space on her card by placing a crayon over the box. When a child has covered all the spaces on her card, she calls out, "Bingo!" and is declared the winner.

This is red. A strawberry is red.

Seat your students in a circle. Play some music and pass around a box of crayons containing the eight basic colors. Stop the music and have the child holding the box pull out one crayon. Have him identify its color and name something that is that color. For example, a child might say, "This is red. A strawberry is red." Ask him to take the crayon and a sheet of paper and go to a table to draw a picture of the object he named. Continue with new boxes of crayons until all the children have drawn pictures. Display the children's pictures. Add new pictures to the display the next time you play this game.

Instant Activities With...
JUMP ROPES

ideas contributed by Suzanne Moore

Use jump ropes to mark off observation areas for your young scientists. Let each pair or small group of children take a jump rope outside and lay it on the ground in a closed circle. Have the children carefully observe the plants and animals inside their jump-rope areas. Encourage them to discuss what they see, smell, and hear. Extend this activity by bringing along paper and crayons and asking youngsters to sketch their observations.

Practice language skills with a little rope writing. Invite your students to use jump ropes to form letters, numerals, or shapes. How many ropes are needed to produce each symbol?

Introduce youngsters to the concept of *perimeter* when you measure with jump ropes. Ask your students how many jump ropes they think will be needed to build an imaginary fence around a table or a center area. Demonstrate how to lay the jump ropes in straight lines, end-to-end. If you have enough jump ropes, find the perimeter of your classroom. Or head outdoors to measure a large area such as the sand area or blacktop.

Use two jump ropes to test your students' conservation of length. Simply lay two identical ropes side by side. Be sure that the end of each jump rope has the same baseline and that the ropes are directly next to one another. Ask a child if the ropes are the same length. Then rearrange one of the ropes into a squiggly or bent line, and ask the same child if the ropes are still the same length. If the child responds that the length has changed, you will know that he has not yet conserved length and will need plenty of practice with hands-on materials to help him understand this concept.

Provide each child with a jump rope. Have her lay the jump rope on the floor in a circle. Then give directions for various types of movements, such as "Hop into your circle," "Hop out of your circle," "Stand on one foot inside your circle," or "Jump around your circle."

Hop to it and practice numerical order! Lay each of several jump ropes in a circle—each circle hopping distance from the circle next to it. If you do this activity outdoors, use chalk to label the circles in numerical order from left to right. If you do this activity indoors, write each numeral on a piece of paper, and tape it to the floor or carpet near a circle. Encourage your little ones to hop from circle to circle, counting aloud as they go.

Arrange jump-rope circles in the same fashion as in the previous activity. Ask one child to stand in each circle, and leave one circle empty. Then designate one child to be the Boss. Have the Boss give directions to the children in the circles, such as "Circle 1, trade with Circle 4," or "Circle 3, go to Circle 5." Any child who is ousted from her circle may stand in the empty circle. After a few rounds of careful listening, have the children in the circles sit down, and invite new players and a new Boss to try this game.

Instant Activities With...
Pipe Cleaners

ideas contributed by Barbara Backer and Joyce Montag

Youngsters will love striking pipe-cleaner poses! Use two pipe cleaners to form a stick figure as shown. Then invite one child at a time to pose the stick figure's arms and legs as she desires. Have her show the pipe-cleaner pose to her classmates, who then imitate the pose with their bodies.

Give each child half of a pipe cleaner and ask him to twist it around his index finger to form a wiggly worm shape. Then have him gently slide it off his finger and hold it in his hand. Teach little ones the song below. Ask them to place their pipe-cleaner worms on the body parts mentioned in the song.

(sung to the tune of "London Bridge")

Willy Worm is on my head, on my head, on my head.
Willy Worm is on my head. Dear old Willy.

He crawled quickly to my [arm], to my [arm], to my [arm].
He crawled quickly to my [arm]. Dear old Willy.

(Continue with more verses like the second stanza, substituting other body parts for the underlined word.)

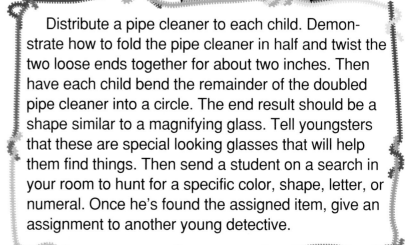

Distribute a pipe cleaner to each child. Demonstrate how to fold the pipe cleaner in half and twist the two loose ends together for about two inches. Then have each child bend the remainder of the doubled pipe cleaner into a circle. The end result should be a shape similar to a magnifying glass. Tell youngsters that these are special looking glasses that will help them find things. Then send a student on a search in your room to hunt for a specific color, shape, letter, or numeral. Once he's found the assigned item, give an assignment to another young detective.

Provide a large supply of pipe cleaners (cut in half, if desired). Have each child form a pattern with some of the pipe cleaners, such as *red, red, blue, red, red, blue.* Then show the children how to twist each pipe cleaner into a circle, and link the pipe cleaners together to make a chain. When each child's chain is long enough, help her open the end links and hook them together to form a necklace. Have each child model her necklace for the class and identify the pattern she created.

Discuss the concept of *camouflage* with your youngsters. Show the children how easy it is to see a red pipe cleaner if it is lying on a white or light-colored background as opposed to a red background. Then let them try this hide-and-seek game.

Divide your class into two groups: the Hiders and the Seekers. Give each Hider a pipe cleaner. As the Seekers cover their eyes, have the Hiders hide their pipe cleaners somewhere in the classroom, attempting to camouflage them. Remind the Hiders that they must leave at least a portion of each pipe cleaner showing. Then invite the Seekers to try to find the camouflaged pipe cleaners. When all the pipe cleaners have been located, have the two groups switch roles.

Have the class help you create a numerals-to-sets matching game to place in your math center. Provide red and white pipe cleaners (cut in half), and invite youngsters to form peppermint sticks or candy canes. Write the numerals one through five on five separate sheets of paper. Put the labeled papers and 15 of the children's candy canes in the center. Invite the students to count out the correct number of candy canes to lay on each numeral. For more advanced students, make a similar game with sets from one through ten.

Ask little ones to twist pipe cleaners to form letters, numerals, or shapes of their choice. Have them share their creations with their classmates. If desired, have children work in pairs. Have one child form a numeral; then have his partner locate the corresponding number of classroom items. Or have one child form a letter; then have his partner find an object in the classroom with that letter's beginning sound.

Instant Activities With... CRACKERS

ideas contributed by Rachel Castro

Pack some learning into snacktime with this edible estimation activity! Give each child a graham cracker, a crayon, and a sheet of paper. Ask each child to estimate how many bites it will take for her to eat her cracker. Write—or ask each child to write—her guess on her paper. Then invite the children to eat their crackers and keep track of how many bites they take. (You may want to have the students use tally marks to record their bites.) Ask each child to write her actual number of bites next to her estimate and compare the two numbers.

If you have a collection of crackers in different shapes, try some shape-identification practice. Give each child at least three crackers in different shapes. Then name a shape and invite everyone to eat a cracker of that shape. Ask student volunteers to name shapes for each round until all the crackers have been consumed.

Use a variety of cracker shapes to practice patterning. Give each student a handful of crackers in a few different shapes. Then draw a pattern that uses these cracker shapes on the board or a sheet of chart paper. Ask a volunteer to name the next shape in the pattern. If a child has a cracker in the named shape, she may eat it. Continue until all the crackers have been eaten.

Give each child a handful of crackers in various shapes. Review the shapes. Then draw a simple picture on your chalkboard, a sheet of chart paper, or the overhead projector. Ask students to use their cracker shapes to copy the picture. (For example, you could draw a simple flower with a circle and a few ovals.) After making several pictures, invite your little artists to eat their materials!

Practice critical thinking with the help of animal crackers. Provide a handful of animal crackers for each youngster. Then give clues about one of the animals, such as "This animal has a mane," or "This animal's name begins with the letter *L.*" After a child correctly guesses the animal, everyone who has a cracker in the shape of that animal may eat it. Continue the activity until everyone has eaten all his crackers.

After a snack of animal crackers, ask the children to vote on their favorite cookie animal. Draw a simple bar graph on your chalkboard or a sheet of chart paper. Ask each child to write her name (or have you write it) in the column beside her favorite animal cracker. Count the names in each column together and discuss the results of your graph. Which animal is the King of the Beasts as far as your students are concerned?

elephant	Rachel, Tia, Kevin, Bobby	4
lion	Steve, Hannah, Robbie	3
monkey	Annie, Shanita, Josh	3
sheep	Phillip	1
zebra	Clifton, Sarah, Zoey	3
giraffe	Chris, Marie	2
camel	Alex	1
tiger		1
olf	Michael, Juan, Carly	3
		2
		1

Have one child stand in front of the class, and give him a full graham cracker. Note for the class that this child has a *whole* graham cracker. Then ask a second child to join him. Ask the class how the two children can share the graham cracker. Discuss any reasonable answers. Guide youngsters to realize that the cracker can be broken into two parts. Break the cracker into two equal pieces and tell students that the name for each of these parts is a *half.* Continue the activity by asking how two more children can also share the cracker. Guide students to discover how the cracker can be broken into *fourths* to be shared. Finish the activity by dividing your class into groups of four. Ask each group to evenly divide a whole graham cracker and eat up their fractions!

Use animal crackers to get sorting skills on the right track. Divide a large box of animal crackers among a large or small group of children. Have students call out the names of the animals they have as you write each animal's name on a separate sheet of paper. Then lay the papers side by side on a long table to represent the cars of a train. Instruct the children to sort their animal crackers into the appropriate train cars. When all the animals are on board the train, count to see how many are in each car. If desired, try this activity with a second box of animal crackers. Compare the number of each type of animal in the two boxes.

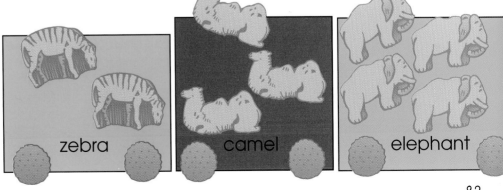

zebra   camel   elephant

Instant Activities With...
BEADS AND LACES

ideas contributed by Ada Goren and Mary Kathryn Martell

The bright colors and varied shapes of wooden beads make them a natural tool for teaching sorting skills. Divide your class into several groups. Give each group a cupful of beads and ask students to sort them by stringing all the like colors (or shapes) onto individual laces. When all the beads are sorted and strung, ask the children to count the beads on each lace. Encourage them to compare which lace has the *most,* which has the *fewest,* and/or which has *equal* numbers of beads.

For higher-level sorting skills, introduce more advanced learners to a Venn diagram. Tape two sheets of construction paper together; then use a marker to draw two interlocking circles on the enlarged paper. Choose two attributes, label the circles accordingly, and have students sort a collection of wooden beads into the corresponding circles. Point out the overlapping area. Show the children how to place all the beads that share *both* attributes into the overlapping area. Point out that any beads left outside the two circles do not share *either* attribute.

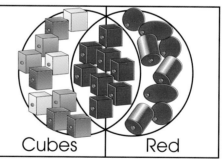

Cubes   Red

How about some partnered patterning practice? Ask each young-ster to pick a partner. Then give each pair a selection of beads and two laces. Ask one child to string beads onto her lace to create a pattern, such as *red cube, yellow sphere, red cube, yellow sphere.* Then have her partner copy the pattern onto his own lace. (Give children with less pattern-ing ability a smaller selection of colors and shapes, and make sure each pair has enough beads to repeat a pattern.)

Give each child a lace and set out a large supply of beads. Ask each child to string several beads onto her lace; then assist the children in tying their laces around their wrists to make bracelets. Then ask everyone to sit in a circle. Begin a color-recognition activity by giving commands, such as "If you have a red bead in your bracelet, stand up," or "If you have a blue bead in your bracelet, put your hands on your head." Continue by identifying other colors and actions for the children to perform.

Make an inclined plane by propping a sheet of poster board or a big book against a table or shelf. Then invite youngsters to experiment with sending beads down your makeshift slide. Have a child place a bead at the top of the slide, then watch to see if it rolls or slides to the floor. After every child has had a chance to send a bead down the slide, ask the children to speculate on why the beads slid or rolled. Guide them to notice the differences in the beads' shapes.

Provide beads and laces for the children in a small group. Give each child a quantity from one to five and ask him to string beads onto his lace to create a corresponding set. Then ask the children to lay their bead-ed lengths side by side and order them from shortest to longest.

Young children love to give gifts to their teacher! Invite them to make a bead necklace for you with this fun review. Begin with an empty lace and a supply of beads. Ask a question to review the skill of your choice—beginning sounds, shapes, colors, or numbers. When someone answers the question correctly, invite him to add a bead to the lace. At the end of your session, tie the resulting necklace around your neck and wear it proudly to show off your youngsters' knowledge!

Instant Activities With...
PUZZLES

ideas contributed by Jan Brennan and Linda Gordetsky

If you have a jigsaw puzzle with a number of pieces that approximately equals the number of children in your group, try this cooperative activity. (Floor puzzles will work well for this activity.) Randomly distribute one puzzle piece to each child. Have the children walk around the classroom looking for someone whose piece will fit with theirs. Once they've made a pair, have them continue to add classmates' pieces until the puzzle is complete.

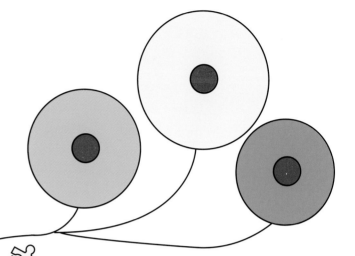

Gather one wooden puzzle for each child in your group. Place the puzzles on the floor in a circle. Play some music and have the children walk around the circle of puzzles. When you stop the music, ask each child to sit down and empty the puzzle closest to him from its frame, then begin to reassemble it. Restart the music after a few minutes and have youngsters walk around the circle until the music stops again. If a child sits in front of a completed puzzle, have her put that puzzle away, and then help a friend finish his puzzle. Continue until all the puzzles are complete and put away.

Divide your class into small groups. Give each group a puzzle to complete. Once they are finished, have the group make up a story about the picture. Write each group's dictated story on a sheet of paper. Share the stories with the class.

Have each child practice her fine-motor and visual-perception skills with this puzzling art activity. Give each child a wooden picture puzzle with a small number of pieces. (Puzzles with knobbed pieces will work especially well for this activity.) Instruct each child to remove each puzzle piece and trace around it on a sheet of paper, attempting to re-create the picture on the puzzle. Invite youngsters to color their finished copies.

Place five puzzles on a table in front of your group. Ask all the children to close their eyes. Randomly remove one piece from each puzzle. Then ask the children to open their eyes. Hand the five puzzle pieces to five of the children. Ask each youngster to find the puzzle to which his piece belongs. Repeat the activity until every child has had a turn.

Divide your class into two teams for this game. Choose two wooden puzzles with approximately the same number of pieces. Show the puzzles to the children; then have all the members on both teams close their eyes while you hide all the puzzle pieces (from both puzzles) around the classroom. Encourage the youngsters to open their eyes and search for the puzzle pieces. Have them deposit found pieces into a central bowl or basket. When all the pieces have been found, choose one or two players from each team to come to the bowl or basket and try to sort out all the pieces that belong in their team's puzzle. Then have each group try to assemble its puzzle. Children may periodically visit the central bowl to return unneeded pieces or take pieces left there by the other team. The first team to complete its puzzle is the winner!

Collect some jigsaw puzzle pieces to make beautiful artwork! Give each child a few puzzle pieces, a sheet of paper, and some crayons. Demonstrate how to place the puzzle pieces under the paper and color over the paper to make a rubbing. Encourage each child to use different colors and move her puzzle pieces to different spots under the paper to make a colorful design.

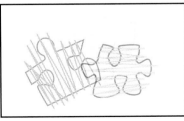

Instant Activities With...
Two-Sided Counters

ideas contributed by Angie Kutzer and Linda Ludlow

In front of a small group of children, display a row of counters in alternating colors. As you point to each counter, direct students to clap for the odd-numbered counters (all one color) and to count aloud the even-numbered counters (the other color). What a simple way to teach rhythm, skip counting, color recognition, even and odd numbers, and patterning!

Designate a motion to correspond with each color represented on your counters. For example, you might tell students to hop for white and flap their arms for blue. Have each child flip a counter; then encourage the rest of the class to perform the corresponding motion. Change the motions periodically using children's suggestions.

Have children stand in a circle. Give one child a two-sided counter and ask her to predict what color the counter will show if she flips it. Then have her flip the counter. If her prediction is correct, she remains standing. If her prediction is incorrect, she sits down. Continue around the circle, giving each child a turn to predict and flip until one child remains standing.

Encourage each student to use counters to form letters, numerals, or the outlines of geometrical shapes. Practice size relationships by having the child make a larger uppercase letter than the lowercase version.

Count on this idea to get students ready for addition. Have a volunteer shake and spill five counters onto a tabletop. On a piece of paper, draw colored dots to record the resulting combination of colors (for example: two yellow, three red). Have another volunteer shake and spill the counters again; then record the combination. Continue until all of the combinations are discovered. Challenge more advanced students to repeat this procedure using a different number of counters.

5

Divide students into pairs for this comparison game. Give each pair of students a handful of two-sided counters. Have each partner choose a different color represented on the counters. To play the game, one of the partners shakes the counters in his hands, then lets them fall on the table. Each player takes the counters that are showing his color. Each player counts his counters, then compares the number to his partner's total to determine the winner of the round. Play continues with the other partner shaking and dropping the counters.

Create a pattern with two-sided counters on a tabletop where children can see it. Have each student use counters to copy and extend your pattern. Invite more advanced youngsters to create patterns for their classmates to copy and extend.

Scatter a handful of counters in front of each child. Have the child sort the counters by color, then arrange each color of counters in a line. Direct the child to match the colors one to one. Then ask the child which color group has more or fewer counters. Repeat the activity by having the child gather his counters, shake them up, and disperse them onto his table again.

Instant Activities With...
Paper Plates

ideas contributed by Barbara Backer

Reinforce letter recognition and lay the foundation for arranging letters alphabetically with this activity for older preschoolers and kindergartners. Give each child two paper plates. Ask him to write one of his favorite letters on each plate. Then recite the alphabet together—slowly—and invite youngsters to lay their plates on the floor in a line as their letters are mentioned. Examine the results. Are any letters missing? Which letters were most popular? Ask some volunteers to write the missing letters on paper plates; then leave the set of plates in your language center so children can play with them.

Children will love acting out a story when no one has to wait for her turn and everyone gets to be her favorite character! Invite youngsters to dramatize a favorite story that they know well, such as *The Three Bears* or *The Three Billy Goats Gruff.* Have each child choose a part she'd like to play and draw a mask of that character on a paper plate. (It's not necessary to cut eyeholes in the masks.) Don't worry if there are four Goldilocks characters or if no one wants to be the middle Billy Goat Gruff. Narrate the story as youngsters hold their masks in front of their faces and act out their parts. Let the actions be spontaneous, and have fun!

Fine-motor skills will be blooming when your little ones transform paper plates into beautiful flowers! Encourage each child to use crayons and scissors to fashion a flower of his choice from a thin paper plate. Display the finished flowers on a bulletin board with construction-paper stems and leaves. If desired, invite each child to name his flower creation.

Make a set of paper-plate puzzles. Ask each child to color a striped pattern on a paper plate. Then cut each plate in half with a jagged or curvy line. Lay all the resulting puzzle pieces on the floor. Invite each of your little ones in turn to choose a piece and find its match.

Give your youngsters a little background information about bats. Point out that while many people think bats are scary, bats eat insects that can be troublesome to people. Then invite your students to create bats from paper plates and brown construction paper. Have each child color a paper plate brown and draw a face on it. Then demonstrate how to cut a sheet of brown construction paper in half diagonally. Help each child staple or tape his paper halves to the sides of his plate to create the bat's wings. When the bats are complete, invite the children to recite this poem:

Some people think I'm scary.
But I'm your friend, it's true.
I eat little mosquitoes
So they won't bite you!

For a wintry craft, give each child three white paper plates, and help him staple or tape them together to form a snowman. Provide crayons so children can decorate their snowmen as desired. Teach youngsters the poem below; then display the snowmen on a bulletin board with a copy of the poem.

I saw a little snowman
Sitting in the sun one day.
I said, "Mr. Snowman,
Won't you please come and play?"
But he only stood there;
In one place he stayed—
Waiting in the sun until
He melted all away.

Make some paper-plate pockets that can be used for a variety of activities. Have each child fold and then cut a paper plate in half. Assist her in stapling or taping the rounded edges to create a pocket. Then try any of the following:

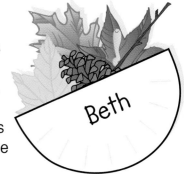

- Go on a nature walk and invite youngsters to collect interesting finds in their pockets. Encourage them to share their collections when you return to the classroom.
- Ask each child to color her pocket with the hue of her choice. Then go on a color hunt around your classroom. Have each child find small items in her chosen color to place inside her pocket. Invite the children to share their collections, then replace the items.
- Have one child at a time place an object in her paper-plate pocket as everyone else closes their eyes. Then have her answer questions about the mystery object as her classmates try to guess what it is.

91

Instant Activities With... DRIED BEANS

ideas contributed by Angie Kutzer and Dawn Spurck

Set out a variety of beans in different shapes, sizes, and colors. Invite each child to choose some of the beans and glue them to a sheet of paper to create an interesting mosaic design.

Use beans to help little ones practice fine-motor skills. For each child, draw a letter, numeral, or shape on a sheet of paper. Have each child trace the figure by placing beans end-to-end on its outline. If desired, direct the child to glue the beans to the outline.

Challenge each child to stack large, flat beans on top of one another to make a tower. When the tower falls, have the child count the number of beans she used. Challenge her to build a taller tower using more beans.

Give each child five beans. Have him set four beans in front of him and hold one bean on his open palm. Invite students to sing the following counting song while manipulating their beans:

Counting Beans
(sung to the tune of "Frère Jacques")

I have one bean. I have one bean.
Yes, I do. Yes, I do.
Here is another, just like the other.
I have two. I have two.

I have two beans. I have two beans.
Yessirree. Yessirree.
Here is another, just like the others.
I have three. I have three.

I have three beans. I have three beans.
Beans galore. Beans galore.
Here is another, just like the others.
I have four. I have four.

I have four beans. I have four beans.
Sakes alive! Sakes alive!
Here is another, just like the others.
I have five. I have five.

I have five beans. I have five beans.
So do you. So do you.
I don't want another, just like the others.
I'm all through. I'm all through.

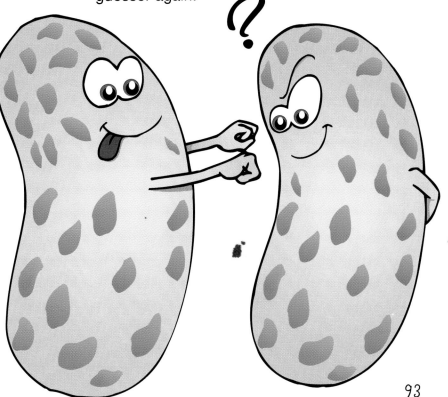

Encourage youngsters to take turns with their partners while playing this bean game. Give each pair of children a handful of beans. Use a narrow permanent marker to draw a happy face on one side of one remaining bean. To play the game, place the additional beans for each pair between the children. Each child in turn shakes the marked bean in her hand and drops it on the table. If the bean lands with the face showing, the child takes a bean from the middle. If the bean's face doesn't show, the child has to put one of her beans back in the middle. (If she has no beans to put in the middle, her turn is over.) The game ends when one of the partners has collected five beans.

Pair your little ones again for this traditional guessing game. Designate one of the partners to go first. Give him a bean. Instruct him to put his hands behind his back and choose one hand in which to hold the bean. Then have him show his closed fists to his partner. Invite his partner to guess which hand the bean is in. Have the child open his hands to check the guess. If the partner is correct, she gets a turn to hide the bean. If she is incorrect, she is the guesser again.

Demonstrate how to balance a bean on your fingertip (or on two fingertips according to the bean's size). Then divide your class into teams for a balance-the-bean race. Instruct one member from each team to walk to a designated area, then back to his team while balancing a bean. If the bean falls during the walk, the child must stop and balance it again before proceeding. The child passes the bean to the next walker for his team. Continue until all team members have had a turn.

Present your little ones with a class supply of beans. Turn on your acting ability as you explain to students that these beans are magic! Tell youngsters that the beans will enable them to change into other people or animals. Give each child a bean and a chance to dramatize whom or what his bean turned him into—maybe a baseball player or an elephant. Abracadabra!

Instant Activities With...
Nature Items

ideas contributed by Jan Brennan and Ada Goren

Take your children on a walk to collect items for some nature collages. Before you start out, give each child a sheet of heavy paper. Take along a few bottles of glue, too. When a student spies an item he'd like to place on his collage—such as a leaf, a blade of grass, or a tiny twig—just squeeze a spot of glue onto his paper and have him begin creating his collage then and there. Return to your classroom and let all the glue dry thoroughly before students share their nature collages with their classmates and families.

Set out an assortment of rocks. Ask young-sters to explore different ways to make sounds with the rocks, such as tapping them on the floor or hitting them together. Then play a selection of lively music and ask your youngsters to form a rock band and play along!

Gather some pebbles and small rocks in vari-ous sizes and shapes. Then set your water table or a large plastic tub filled with water in an outdoor play area. Invite your little ones to ex-periment with dropping the pebbles and rocks into the water. Direct their attention to the differ-ences in ripples and splashes made by each rock. Count the seconds to see how long the ripples last when a small pebble is dropped as opposed to a larger rock.

Young children will be fascinated by the "magic" of leaf rubbings. Have your students help you gather some large leaves in various shapes. Then show them how to place a leaf under a sheet of paper, then rub over the paper with a crayon until the shape of the leaf ap-pears. Invite each child to make a rubbing of one or more leaves, using different crayon col-ors. Display this lovely leaf artwork in your classroom for all to see.

Writing takes on new excitement when it's done with a stick in the sand. Invite each child to find a suitable stick to use to practice his "sandwriting" in your outdoor play area. Then encourage the children to practice writing their names or forming letters, numerals, and shapes.

Encourage your students to compare the many textures found in nature. Take your students outside and ask them to touch several different surfaces, such as branches of shrubbery, the bark of a tree, a patch of thick grass, and a sandy play area. Elicit descriptive language as your class visits each area. Which things feel soft? Which things feel rough?

Take your little ones on a walk to hunt for animal homes. Take along a clipboard and pencil, and record all the animal homes your children spot. Before you begin, review some animal homes the children can look for—such as birds' and bees' nests, anthills, spiderwebs, or even butterfly and moth cocoons. Remind the children not to touch any of the animal dwellings. When you return to the classroom, read the list and see how many animal homes the class found. Bet you have a lot of neighbors!

For this small-group game, have your students help you gather a collection of smooth pebbles or round nuts. Use chalk or tape to outline a circle on a sidewalk or your classroom floor. Group all the pebbles or nuts in the center, as in a game of marbles. Then have a child drop one pebble or nut into the group to make them scatter. The child may then gather and keep all the pebbles or nuts that roll or bounce outside the circle. Gather the remaining pebbles or nuts and group them in the center again. Then invite another child to play. Continue until all the pebbles or nuts are taken. Then have the children count to see who has the most.

birds' nests
bees' nests
anthills
spiderwebs
cocoons
squirrels' nests
wasps' nests

Instant Activities With...
PLAY DOUGH

ideas contributed by Barbara Backer and Mackie Rhodes

Nourish students' food knowledge with this categorization activity. Give each child some play dough. Explain that you will name a food category, such as vegetables, meat, or bread. Then have each child form her dough into the shape of a food belonging in that category. Invite each child in turn to tell which food she created; then repeat the activity using a different food category. It's fat-free, sugar-free fun!

Here's an idea you can count on for practice in numeral formation and number concepts! Group youngsters into pairs; then give each child some play dough. Ask one child in each pair to roll her dough into a rope, then form the rope into a numeral shape. Have her partner create an equal number of balls from her dough. Then have the pair count the balls together to check. Repeat the procedure, inviting the partners to switch roles.

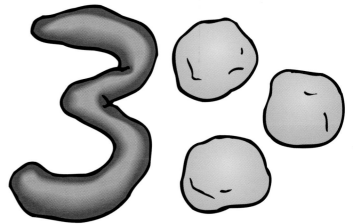

Give youngsters the opportunity to make predictions with this "pet-pourri" project. To begin, give each child some play dough and have each child fashion a pet animal—such as a dog, cat, fish, bird, mouse, rabbit, or snake—from his play dough. Then encourage each child, in turn, to show his pet creation to the class. Challenge the other students to identify the animal. If the class has difficulty guessing, ask the child to give one clue about his dough pet at a time until someone correctly identifies it.

Fascinate youngsters with the color creations that result when different colors of play dough are combined. Have each child form a few small balls from several different play-dough colors; then ask him to group the balls closely together on a table. Have the child use the palm of one hand to press the balls together, forming a large patty from the flattened balls. What new colors were created? Ask the child to continue pressing the dough and working it with his fingers to create as many different colors as possible. Red, blue, yellow, and white make a colorful play-dough sight!

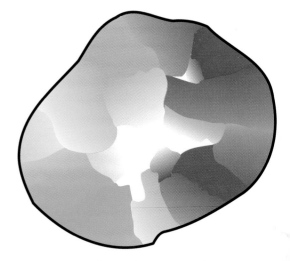

Furnish youngsters with more than just fine-motor practice with this activity. Name a room in a house; then have each child design a play-dough model of a piece of furniture that might be found in that room. Encourage her to add details and decorative touches to personalize her creation. Then invite each child to show and tell about her masterpiece. Such delightful designs!

Produce a chain of positive statements with this self-esteem booster. To begin, roll a portion of play dough into a rope; then ask each child to make a rope with her own portion of dough. Shape your rope into a loop to resemble a chain link as you tell the class something positive about yourself, such as "I'm a very good Rollerblader®." Then have each child, in turn, do the same, looping her rope through a previously formed link so that a chain is created. If desired, allow the completed chain to dry for several days; then display it as a reminder of class members' positive points.

Snip away at those extra classroom moments with this quick tip. Give each child a portion of play dough and a pair of scissors. Have the child form his dough into a ball or patty, then cut out a shape—such as a cube or triangle—from the dough. Or have him cut a dough rope into small pieces. Both youngsters and *you* will enjoy this kind of cutting up!

There's no disguising the emotions that little ones will experience when they create these play-dough masks. Have each child create a large dough patty; then instruct him to form eye, nose, and mouth openings in the patty to create a face mask that represents an emotion, such as *happy, sad, angry,* or *scared.* Invite each child to take a turn holding his mask to his face and then describing the emotion it represents.

Squeeze in a fine-motor workout for students with this lively ditty. Give each child a portion of play dough; then have her perform the action mentioned in this chant. Each time you repeat the chant, replace the underlined action word with one of the following: *roll, poke, pound, pinch,* or *stretch.*

(chanted to the rhythm of "Peanut, Peanut Butter")

You take your lump of play dough and you [squeeze] it, you [squeeze] it.
You [squeeze] it, [squeeze] it, [squeeze] it!

Play dough. You can [squeeze] it—*(whisper)* [squeeze] it!
Play dough. You can [squeeze] it—*(whisper)* [squeeze] it!

A "hole" lot of learning will be accomplished with these play-dough doughnuts. To begin, have each child form his portion of dough into a ring resembling a doughnut. Then divide your class into small groups of students. Ask each group to stack its doughnuts according to size so that the smallest one is on top of the stack. Or expand this into a whole-class learning activity by having youngsters establish a stacked color pattern with their doughnuts and then repeating this pattern until all the doughnuts have been used. This idea is stacked with potential!

Accessorize your class's extra time by giving youngsters the opportunity to role-play creative craftspeople. Give each child a quantity of play dough to fashion into a piece of jewelry, such as a ring, bracelet, or necklace. Encourage him to use bits of different dough colors to embellish his creation. Now that's a flattering piece of work!

Want to know a secret? This activity is ideal for practicing deductive-reasoning skills! Group your class into pairs; then give each student pair a portion of play dough and some crayons. Invite one child from each pair to completely wrap a crayon in a dough patty out of her partner's view. Ask that child to give clues to her partner about the crayon's color—such as "Bananas are this color," or "This color is in the teacher's shirt"—until the partner guesses the color. Then have the guesser unwrap the crayon to check her response. Repeat the game, having the partners switch roles. The secret's out!

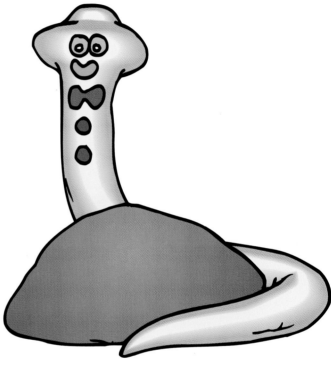

"Snakes" alive! Youngsters will wriggle with enthusiasm as they show off their positional knowledge in this activity. To begin, have each child create a dough patty to represent a flat rock and a dough rope to represent a snake. Then instruct students to move their snakes according to your directions, such as "Crawl around the rock," "Slither to the left of the rock," "Wriggle under the rock," or "Slide over the rock." With this idea, students are positioned for success-s-s-s!

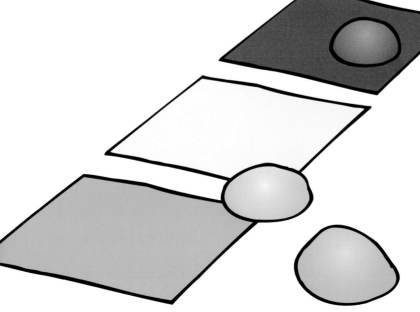

Target color matching and eye-hand coordination with this idea. Create a tape line on the floor; then, at a desired distance, position a different-colored sheet of construction paper to represent each play-dough color to be used. Give each child a portion of dough to roll into a ball. Then challenge each child, in turn, to stand at the line and either toss or roll his ball onto the corresponding sheet of paper.

Instant Activities With...
Dominoes

ideas contributed by Linda Gordetsky

Prepare this special delivery activity in a flash. Draw a very simple house shape on each of 12 sheets of paper. Number each house with a numeral from 1 to 12. Then ask a youngster to play the part of the mail carrier. Explain that the dominoes represent pieces of mail that need to be delivered to the numbered houses. Invite the mail carrier to pick a domino from a box or basket. Have her count the number of dots on the domino. Then invite her to "deliver" the domino mail to the house with the corresponding numeral. Continue with other children playing the part of the mail carrier until interest wanes.

Divide your class into pairs and give each pair a few dominoes. Have one child in each pair hide one domino in her hand. Ask the other child to guess how many dots are on the hidden domino. Then have the hider show the domino, and invite the guesser to check his guess by counting the dots on the domino. If he guessed correctly, he may keep the domino. If he was incorrect, his partner may keep it. Then have the children switch roles. Continue play until all the dominoes are in a child's possession.

To vary the game described above, have the guesser guess whether the number of dots on the hidden domino is fewer than five or more than five. (If desired, designate a higher number for older children or for those with better counting skills.)

If your students are not already familiar with the game of dominoes, explain that dominoes can be laid next to each other only if the sets of dots on the ends that touch are equal. Demonstrate this for them. Then—using this requirement—challenge youngsters to lay dominoes out in the shape of a rectangle or a square.

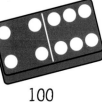

Try a game of domino bowling. On one end of a rectangular tabletop, set up ten dominoes to resemble bowling pins. Then invite a child to slide another domino or roll a small ball from the opposite end of the table and try to knock down as many dominoes as possible. Give each child two attempts to knock down all the pins, just as in a real bowling game.

Use dominoes to get your little ones moving *and* counting. Have one child stand in front of the rest of the group. Have him choose a domino from a box or basket and count the number of dots on it. But tell him not to show or tell the number of dots to the class. Ask him to choose a specific movement—such as toe touches, jumping jacks, or hops—and perform it the same number of times as there are dots on the domino. Have the rest of the class count as he exercises to determine how many dots are on his domino. Continue with other volunteers and dominoes as time permits.

Divide your class into two teams for this relay race. Have each team line up with one child behind another. Provide a box for each team, and place the boxes an equal distance from the two lines of children. Give the leader of each line a domino. Then set a timer and give the starting signal. The first child on each team begins passing the domino overhead until it reaches the last child in line. That child runs to the designated box and deposits the domino, then runs back to the start of the line and gets another domino from you. Have each team continue in this manner until the timer rings. Then have all members of each team sit down and help count the total number of dots on all the dominoes their team collected in the box. The team with the most dots wins!

Older kindergartners will enjoy this activity involving number combinations. Draw a number of blank dominoes on your chalkboard or a sheet of chart paper. Then instruct a child to pick a domino from a box or basket. Have her count the number of dots on the domino and announce the total, but not show the domino to the other children. Ask for volunteers to come up and draw a possible arrangement of dots that would equal the total given. The child whose drawing matches the chosen domino wins the round and gets to pick the next domino. 101

Instant Activities With...
Rubber Stamps
and
Ink Pads

ideas contributed by Vicki Pacchetti

 Provide each child with a sheet of paper, a selection of rubber stamps, and access to an ink pad. Have him choose two or three rubber stamps to stamp onto his paper. Then ask him to make up a story about the resulting picture. As you circulate to write each child's dictation, have the other students use crayons to add details to their illustrations. You're sure to hear some "stamping-good" stories!

This idea is as easy as A-B-C! Label each of 26 sheets of paper with a different letter of the alphabet. Then encourage each student to select a rubber stamp, identify the image on it, and name its beginning sound. Have her stamp the picture onto the paper labeled with the corresponding letter. When you've exhausted your rubber-stamp collection, bind these pages together behind a cover that reads "Our Rubber-Stamp Alphabet." Add this class book to your reading area.

Use letter stamps to help children practice spelling their own and their friends' names. Provide ink pads, letter stamps, paper, and—if desired—a class list. Then encourage youngsters to spell and stamp away!

Some long strips of paper, ink pads, and a selection of rubber stamps are all you need to practice patterning. Have each child choose two or three stamps. Then either begin a pattern and have the child extend it, or have each child create her own pattern, stamping the paper strip from end to end. When she's done, fit the strip around her head, and staple or tape it in place. If you have time, take your youngsters on a Pattern Parade down the hallway!

Invite youngsters to make individual counting books. First decide what numbers you'd like your age group to work on. A book of numbers from one through five will be appropriate for younger children. Older kindergartners might want to stamp ten pages with ten pictures each to make a book of 100 pictures! After you've decided, cut sheets of paper into halves or fourths; then staple together the appropriate number of sheets for each child. Have each student label her pages with the appropriate numbers, then stamp corresponding sets of pictures on each page.

Have each child make a personalized Concentration game to practice visual-memory skills. Provide each of your little ones with a supply of two-inch paper squares, a selection of rubber stamps, and access to ink pads. Ask each child to choose a stamp and stamp it (using the same ink color) on two squares of paper. Have her continue using different stamps to make pairs of pictures until she has a number of squares appropriate for your age group. Then encourage each child to play a game of Concentration, either alone or with a partner.

Give each child a sheet of paper. Set out ink pads and a variety of rubber stamps. Ask each child to choose a stamp and stamp up to ten pictures on her paper. Then have all the children bring their papers to your circle area. Call out two children's names and have them stand in front of the group. Say either, "More," or "Less," and ask the two children to compare the quantities on their papers. If you said, "More," the child with more pictures on her paper remains standing and the other sits down. (Likewise, if you said, "Less," the child with fewer pictures remains standing.) Call another child and again say, "More," or "Less." Continue this activity as along as interest dictates.

Use stamps to complete a class rebus story. First select several rubber stamps that could be used as the basis of the story—perhaps a pumpkin, a Pilgrim, a turkey, and a tree. On a sheet of chart paper, begin writing the story. Demonstrate how to add a rubber-stamp picture in place of a word. Encourage the children to help you complete the story, inserting rubber-stamp illustrations in place of the words where possible. Engage the youngsters in reading the finished story together.

Instant Activities With...
TOY VEHICLES

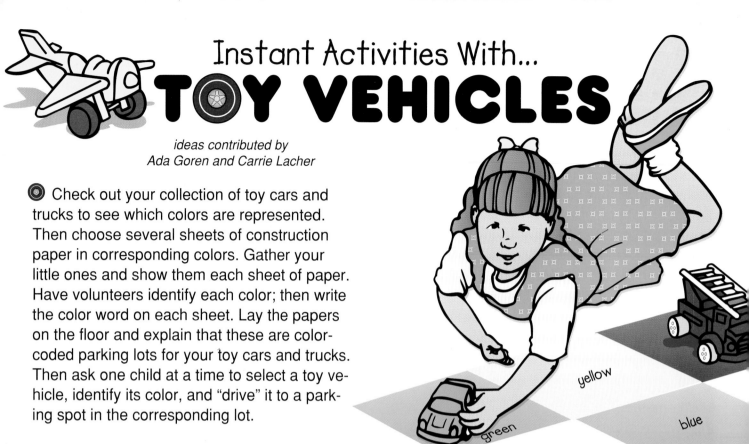

ideas contributed by
Ada Goren and Carrie Lacher

◎ Check out your collection of toy cars and trucks to see which colors are represented. Then choose several sheets of construction paper in corresponding colors. Gather your little ones and show them each sheet of paper. Have volunteers identify each color; then write the color word on each sheet. Lay the papers on the floor and explain that these are color-coded parking lots for your toy cars and trucks. Then ask one child at a time to select a toy vehicle, identify its color, and "drive" it to a parking spot in the corresponding lot.

◎ Invite youngsters to use toy cars and trucks to demonstrate their knowledge of opposites. Have each child select a vehicle. Then give a command, such as "Drive your car *up* a hill," and have children dramatize this action. Then give a command to do the opposite: "Drive your car *down* a hill." Continue with other opposites, such as *stop/go, right/left,* and *on/off.* If your children are already adept at opposites, increase the difficulty of the activity by asking them to perform *only* the opposite of your command. For example, if you say, "Drive your car *fast,"* they should drive their cars *slowly.*

◎ Merge imaginative play with real life when you take youngsters on a vehicle walk. Before starting out, distribute a toy vehicle to each child in your group. Have each child look at her toy and note its color and the type of vehicle it represents (car, truck, fire engine, bus, etc.). Then take a walk near your school to see how many children can find real-life matches for their toys. Take along a pencil and paper and note all the matches that are found. Review the list when you return to the classroom. Invite children to remain on the lookout as they travel to and from school over the following days. It probably won't be long until everyone has found a realistic counterpart to her toy vehicle.

Martin found a
blue car.

Donnie found a
bulldozer.

Camille saw a fire
engine.

water

◉ Remind your students that all vehicles travel by land, by air, or by water. Label three sheets of paper—one with waves and the word "water," one with clouds and the word "air," and one with a road and grass and the word "land." Then invite your youngsters to classify your toy vehicles into these three groups. Have one child at a time select a vehicle and place it near the corresponding sheet of paper. When all the vehicles are sorted, ask the children to count to determine which group has the most vehicles.

◉ This team game is a gas! Divide your class into teams of five. Have each team form a line, with a wide space between each child. Give the first child in each line a car. Explain that in order to fill his tank with gas, he must correctly answer a question you ask. Ask questions to help children review shapes, colors, beginning sounds, or any skill of your choice. If the child answers correctly, he may roll the gassed-up car to the next player. Continue asking questions until someone on that team misses. Then move to the next team and begin at the front of the line. Continue until all the cars have traveled the length of their lines.

◉ If you're a little tired of singing "The Wheels On The Bus," give the song new life by substituting the name and features of another vehicle. Choose a different vehicle from your toy collection, such as a fire truck. Have the children help you brainstorm possible verses for the song. "The siren on the fire truck goes 'Whoo-oo-oo'…"

◉ Toy cars are the perfect vehicles for practice with ordinal numbers. Ask three children at a time to come to the front of your group. Give each child a toy vehicle and ask the youngsters to place the cars in a line. Have them identify which cars are *first, second,* and *third.* Then invite the children to "race" their cars. Mark a start and a finish line on the floor with chalk or tape. Have the participants stand behind the starting line, holding their toy vehicles. On the starting signal, have them run to the finish line. Identify which racers came in *first, second,* and *third.* Then repeat the lineup and race with other groups of children.

Instant Activities With... Chairs

ideas contributed by Linda Gordetsky and Angie Kutzer

Good observation skills are needed for this fun game. Choose one volunteer to be It. Direct the rest of the students to sit in their chairs in a circle so that their backs face the middle of the circle. To play the game, It walks around the outside of the circle while the group sings the following tune:

(sung to the tune of "Go In And Out The Window")

> Go 'round and 'round the circle,
> Go 'round and 'round the circle,
> Go 'round and 'round the circle,
> Now stop and close your eyes.

It closes his eyes and a volunteer leaves the circle and hides. Then It opens his eyes and walks around the circle while the rest of the group sings the tune again, this time substituting "Now who has disappeared?" for the last line. It tries to guess who's missing. He keeps guessing until the guess is correct; then the child who hid becomes It for the next round.

Youngsters will go wild over this activity involving positional words and phrases. Have each child take her chair to an empty space in the room. Explain to the children that they are lions in the circus and that you are their trainer. Direct the children to listen closely to your directions, then act them out. Give commands such as "Get under the chair," "Go around the chair two times," "Jump beside the chair," and "Squat behind the chair." Little ones will roar for more!

Add a twist to the traditional game of Musical Chairs. Instead of removing a chair each time the music stops, direct the child who is left without a seat to name a song or rhyme of his choice. Have the class perform the song or rhyme before starting the music again. What an exciting musical review!

Arrange a class supply of chairs in a circle and direct each child to take a seat. Display a number of objects in the middle of the circle. Instruct a volunteer—the Guesser—to close her eyes. Have another volunteer place one of the objects under the Guesser's chair, then cover the rest of the collection with a large sheet of paper or a child's rest towel. The Guesser then opens her eyes and asks the group questions, using her problem-solving abilities to guess which item is under her chair. If the Guesser has difficulty guessing or asking questions, invite the group to give her clues about the chosen object. Continue until each child has had a turn to guess.

Coordination, gross-motor, and counting skills get a workout in this chair activity. Have youngsters sit in their chairs in a close circle. Roll a ball into the circle. Encourage students to take turns gently kicking the ball while counting each kick aloud to keep score. Explain that the game stops when the ball is kicked too hard, hands touch the ball, or the ball leaves the circle. Challenge students to better their score for each round.

Line up the students' chairs one behind another. You're ready for a very memorable train ride! Select a volunteer conductor to sit in the first chair. Have him call out, "All aboard!" to signal the other children to find a seat. After everyone is seated, have the conductor announce the trip by saying, "We're going to the [zoo]. I hope we see a [zebra]." The next child on board continues by saying, "I hope we see a zebra and a [bear]." The game keeps going with each child repeating the list of animals, then adding his own animal to the list. When the list gets too lengthy for a child to remember, change conductors and begin another trip.

Use this chair activity to emphasize the concepts of *first* and *last*. Direct youngsters to arrange their chairs in a straight line, one behind the other; then have them sit down. Start the exercise by saying, "Switch!" On your cue, the first child runs to the last chair while the rest of the group moves up one chair. After everyone is seated, the new first child says, "I'm first!" and the new last child says, "I'm last!" Then the children wait for your cue again. Continue until everyone has had a chance to be first and last.

Instant Activities With...
PAPER AND SCISSORS

ideas contributed by Ada Goren and Angie Kutzer

Begin a shapes review by giving each child a large construction-paper square. Ask him to use his scissors to change the square into a circle. Then ask him to change the circle into a triangle. Continue with other shapes if desired.

Give each child a large paper square folded in half. Explain that you will be making a house from your own square, and encourage children to follow along. Have each child hold his paper so that the fold is at the bottom. Demonstrate how to cut out a door, window, and chimney so that the house looks similar to the one shown. (Provide assistance if necessary.) After everyone completes his house, ask children to guess who might live there. Then invite each little one to unfold his paper to reveal the robot home dweller. Ta-da!

Challenge each child to cut a sheet of paper into five pieces. Then have her arrange the pieces from largest to smallest.

Children will get some estimation practice during this activity. Cut a paper strip for each child. Have her estimate the length of a designated pencil, crayon, or stick by cutting her strip to the estimated length. Ask each child to write her name on her strip, then compare it to the actual object. Whose estimate was closest?

Paper and scissors are all you need to create these crawling critters. Give each child a paper square. (The larger the square, the easier this activity will be.) Have him fold his square in half two times. Then direct him to cut various shapes from all four edges of the square without completely cutting any of the folds—similarly to cutting a decorative snowflake. Encourage him to unfold the paper to reveal the creepy critter he's created.

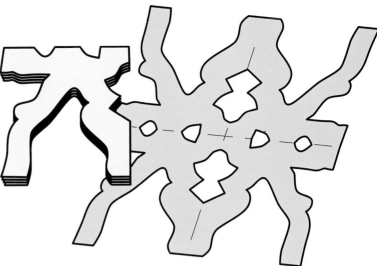

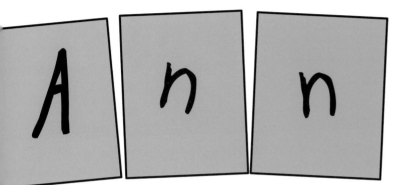

Cut a class supply of paper strips. Have each child write her name on a strip. Instruct the child to cut her strip apart, so that each letter is on a separate slip of paper. Then have her sequence the letters to reassemble her name. For added difficulty, encourage each student to switch name pieces with a classmate.

Students can sharpen their numeration skills with this instant activity. Give each child a piece of paper. Call out a number from one to ten. Have each student cut her paper into the corresponding number of pieces. Check her results; then ask her to clear her workspace except for one of the cut pieces of paper. Call out another number and have her cut the remaining paper into the number of pieces that matches the new number. Continue with one more round of cutting, if desired. Then challenge each youngster to count the total number of paper pieces she cut.

Invite children to use their imaginations to create paper sculptures. First show students how to connect two pieces of paper by cutting a slit in each piece, then sliding the pieces together. Provide colorful scraps of construction paper for children to use in their construction. Display these modern works of art in a tabletop museum.

109

Instant Activities With...
BUTTONS

ideas contributed by Jan Brennan and Angie Kutzer

Glue one button to a piece of paper; then demonstrate some simple drawings that incorporate the button as an object or part of an object in the picture. Then give each child a piece of paper, glue, and some buttons. Encourage her to use one or more of the buttons and her imagination to create her own work of art.

Use chalk or tape to make a line approximately one yard from a wall. Give each child an easily distinguishable button. (If buttons are too much alike, write each child's initials on his button.) Have each child stand behind the line and toss his button against the wall. After everyone has had a turn, compare to see whose button landed closest to the wall. Invite children to collect their buttons and give it another try.

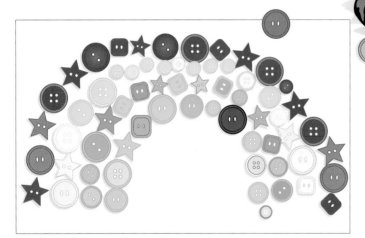

Colors, colors, colors! Have each child sort a handful of buttons by color. Then direct him to glue the buttons onto a sheet of paper in arches to create a unique rainbow. If your button collection isn't large enough for each child to have a handful, have students work in small groups. Or have the whole class work together to create one large rainbow.

Set out your button collection for exploration. Encourage children to try to find as many identical pairs of buttons as they can.

Seat students in a circle and choose a volunteer to be It. Instruct It to close her eyes. Play some music and have students pass a button around the circle. When the music stops, have all of the children hold their clasped hands in front of them. Ask It to open her eyes and guess who has the button. If her guess is correct, she gets to be It again. If her guess is incorrect, the child holding the button gets to be It. For a variation, have students pass more than one button.

Here's a game for small groups that youngsters will flip over! Draw a circle on a piece of construction paper. Put several small buttons in the middle of the circle. Give each player a large button. To play the game, each child takes a turn using his large button to snap down on the edge of a small button in order to make the small button move. Anytime a player makes a small button move to the outside of the drawn circle, he gets to keep the button. When all of the buttons have been moved out of the circle, players count and compare their collections.

Gather a distinct, matching pair of buttons for each student. Keep one button from each of the pairs; then distribute their matches to the children. Have each child study her button. Choose a button to describe to the class. Give one clue at a time, such as "This button is white." Have all the children whose buttons match your clue stand. Continue with additional clues. Direct children to sit when their buttons no longer match your description. When only one child is left standing, reveal the chosen button and have the child compare her button to it to see if they match.

Review body parts with buttons. Give each child a button; then call out directions such as "Put the button in your hand. Put the button on your knee. Put the button on your cheek." For added fun, ask volunteers to make up and call out their own directions for the group to follow.

111

Instant Activities With...
PLASTIC FOOD

ideas contributed by Carrie Lacher

THANK YOU

Use the play food from your dramatic-play center to help children polish their manners. With your class seated in a group, ask two volunteers to stand in front. Ask each child in the pair to select a few foods from your collection. Encourage the volunteers to demonstrate proper manners as they ask for and pass the food items to one another. Remind them to use words such as *please, thank you,* and *you're welcome.* Continue the activity with more volunteers.

If you have any type of large container in your classroom (a tub, a large basket, or a box), you can cook up a pot of imaginary Sharing Soup. Begin by asking each youngster to select a plastic food from your collection. Then gather the children in a circle and ask them to use their imaginations. Have them pretend that they live in a town called "[Your school]land." The weather has been very bad and the food won't grow. Everyone is very hungry, and each person only has a tiny bit of food to eat. Set the large container in the center of the group and suggest that if everyone adds his food to this pot, they can make some Sharing Soup. Invite each child to come up and drop his food into the container; then give everyone a turn to "stir" the soup. Pretend to ladle up a serving for each child as you discuss how good it feels to share!

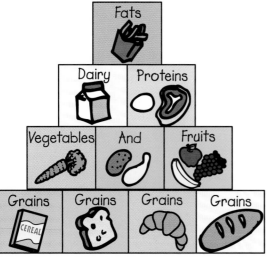

Plastic foods are a natural tool for teaching about the Food Guide Pyramid. Ask little ones to observe as you lay several sheets of construction paper on the floor in the shape of a pyramid. Label each section of the Food Guide Pyramid with the appropriate food group. Then help youngsters select items from your play-food collection and place them on the correct sections of the pyramid. Talk about each food group as you go.

Review with your youngsters the components of a balanced meal. Then ask a few children at a time to select foods from your dramatic-play center that comprise a nutritious meal. Talk about whether each child's choices would make a good breakfast, lunch, or dinner. If desired, extend this activity by having each child illustrate his menu on a sheet of paper.

This song will help little ones practice their classification skills. Have each youngster choose an item from your play-food collection, then join the class in a seated circle. Go around the circle, having each child identify the food she chose and tell what type of food it is (a vegetable, a fruit, a meat, a bread, etc.). Then have the group sing the song below, substituting the child's name and type of food for the underlined words.

(sung to the tune of "Mary Wore Her Red Dress")

[Taylor] has a [fruit], a [fruit], a [fruit].
[Taylor] has a [fruit] at school today.

For some food fun that's sure to get your group giggling, invite youngsters to create some food faces! Have them choose a variety of plastic foods from your collection to represent the eyes, nose, mouth, ears, and even hair of a person. Let's see…brussels-sprout eyes, a bagel nose, and how about a banana mouth?

Try this version of the traditional game Hot Potato to emphasize an important nutrition concept. Rather than passing around a plastic potato, select a junk-food item. Remind youngsters that this is a food we don't want to eat often, because it isn't very good for us. Have the children pass the junk food quickly around the circle. If a child drops it, he must sit in the middle of the circle. Keep going until only one child is left. Then invite all your children to be nutritional winners by selecting a healthful food item from your play-food collection.

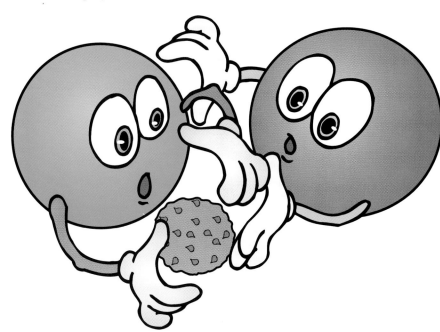

113

Instant Activities With...
PAPER LUNCH BAGS

ideas contributed by Jan Brennan and Ada Goren

Divide your class into two or three teams. Have each team line up with one child behind another. Give the first child on each team an empty paper lunch bag. Across the room from where the teams are lined up, place a basket of crayons on a table. On your starting signal, have each child with a bag run to the basket and count out five crayons to put into his bag. He then runs back to the next child in line who takes the bag and runs back to the basket. She removes all the crayons from the bag and returns the empty bag to the third child in line. Play continues in the same manner. The first team to have all its members run is the winner!

Give each child a paper lunch bag. Have the children follow your directions as you show them how to cut off the bottom of the bag, then make a cut up one side of the remaining bag, so that you have a flat rectangle. Then have each child cut a zigzag design along one edge of the rectangle, creating a flattened crown shape. Provide crayons and invite each youngster to decorate her crown as she desires. Then fit each child's crown around her head, and staple the ends of the crown as shown to create a perfect fit.

Practice eye-hand coordination with some paper-bag basketball. Have each child choose a partner. Give each pair a paper lunch bag and a pair of scissors, and instruct them to cut off the bottom of the bag. Tape the resulting paper hoop to a wall or bulletin board at an accessible height for the children. Have one child in each pair wad the cutoff bag bottom into a paper ball. Then invite the partners to take turns shooting the paper ball. Have the children stand closer or farther away from the goal to vary the difficulty.

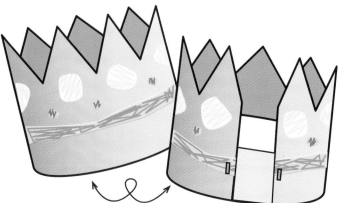

Paper lunch bags are, of course, usually used for lunches! Invite your youngsters to create a class book about their favorite lunch foods. Have each child draw a picture of what he likes to pack in his lunch on a 4" x 9" sheet of construction paper. Then give each child a lunch bag, and ask him to slip his drawing inside it. On the front of each child's bag, write "[Child's name] likes…." On another bag, write the title "What We Like In Our Lunch Bags." Then staple all the bags (the pages) together along the fold as shown with the cover on top. Share the resulting book with your class, removing and showing each child's drawing as you come to his page.

Supply each child with a paper lunch bag and a pair of scissors. Have each youngster cut her bag in half, then open the section of the bag with the bottom still intact. Assist each youngster in cutting a hole large enough to slip her finger into in the bottom of her bag. Then use a fine-tip marker to draw a simple face on each child's index finger. Encourage each child to place her bag over her hand and experiment with slipping her finger in and out of the hole. Then teach your little ones this rhyme and its accompanying actions.

Wiggle worm, wiggle worm,
Where are you?
Here I am! *(Slide finger out of hole.)*
How do you do?
Wiggle to the left; *(Wiggle finger to left.)*
Wiggle to the right; *(Wiggle finger to right.)*
Wiggle, wiggle, wiggle,
With all your might! *(Wiggle finger all around.)*
Uh-oh, uh-oh; here comes the rain!
Wiggle back into your hole again!
(Slide finger back into bag.)

Try a little target practice to help your little ones practice letter, numeral, or shape identification. To begin, position several paper lunch bags with their openings at the bottom. Then draw a different letter, numeral, or shape on each bag. Open the bags and stand them on end in a row. Take another bag and wad it into a ball. Then invite each child, in turn, to identify one of the symbols and throw the paper ball from a specified distance, attempting to knock down the named bag.

Tell the children that they are going to prepare a special gift for their moms and dads. Ask each child to use crayons to decorate a white paper lunch bag as she chooses. (Some children may want to make more than one bag.) Ask each child to "pour" some love from her heart into the empty bag, then fold it closed. Then teach the children this poem to recite when they present their bags to their caregivers. If time permits, copy the poem onto paper and duplicate it for each child to take home with her bag.

Here's a present for you from me.
Can you guess what it might be?
It's something sweet, but not to eat.
It's something nice, without a price.
Look with your heart and not your eyes.
Get ready for a big surprise.
A very special gift, it's true—
This bag is full of LOVE for you!

115

Instant Activities With... Index Cards

ideas contributed by Angie Kutzer and Dawn Spurck

Give each of your little ones an index card. Punch each card with one, two, three, four, or five holes. Then write the numerals one through five on the chalkboard. Direct each child to count the holes in his card and sit in front of the correct numeral. Call out both serious and silly directions for each specific group to follow. For example, you might say, "Number 4s, clap your hands four times. Number 2s, sing 'Twinkle, Twinkle, Little Star.' " After each group has followed one of your directions, take up the cards and redistribute them for another round of listening fun.

Create architectural wonders with index cards. Encourage small groups of students to work together to build index-card houses by stacking and leaning cards together. Which group has the longest house? Which group has the tallest?

Simon

Use index cards to graph children's responses to various questions. Give each child an index card. Have her draw and color a self-portrait on the card, then label her card with her name. Label one sheet of construction paper with "yes" and another sheet of paper with "no." Lay the yes and no papers on the floor to use as graph headings. Ask your group a yes/no question; then have each child respond by placing her index card in a line above or next to the correct heading. Compare the results.

Collect the self-portrait index cards from the activity above. Tape them together accordion-style. Add another index card to the front titled "See My Friends In School." Pass the book around the class; then challenge the children to line up in the same order that they appear in the book. Place the book in your library center for future enjoyment.

Ask each child to decorate an index card with crayons or markers. Roll up the card—decorated side out—and tape the short edges together. Invite youngsters to go on a treasure hunt in your classroom using their magic telescopes to find specific objects, such as something green or something round.

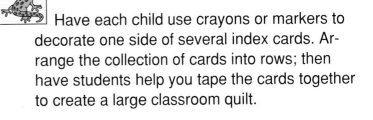

 Label each of five index cards with an *X.* Mix these cards with other plain index cards; then spread out all of the cards on the floor, facedown. Have each child pick a card and turn it over. If the card is plain, she gets to keep it. If the card is marked with an *X,* she returns it and any other collected cards to the cards on the floor, then reshuffles the cards. After everyone has had three turns, count aloud the number of cards each child collected to see who has the most.

Have each child use crayons or markers to decorate one side of several index cards. Arrange the collection of cards into rows; then have students help you tape the cards together to create a large classroom quilt.

Give each child an index card and a half-sheet of construction paper. Have him fold his card in half to resemble a tent. Then help him tape one side of his tent to the center of his construction paper. Direct the child to lift the tent and draw someone or something sleeping inside. Write the name of the child's chosen sleeper on the inside of the tent as shown. After allowing each child to tell about his camping buddy, display the finished projects on a board titled "Who's sleeping in each of our tents?"

Blake

Instant Activities With...
CLOTHESPINS

ideas contributed by Angie Kutzer and Mary Kathryn Martell

Have children work in small groups or with partners to fasten clothespins together to create freestanding imaginative sculptures. Be sure to display these fine-motor masterpieces!

Choose one volunteer to be the Hider. Ask the rest of the group to close their eyes. Instruct the Hider to clip a clothespin somewhere in the room that's visible from where the class is sitting, such as on a window blind or on a pillow in the reading area. Have the children open their eyes and begin the search. Invite the child who names the location of the clothespin to be the next Hider.

Divide your class into four groups (or two groups if you have a small class) and assign each group a color. Give each child a clothespin. Have the children in each group use markers to color their clothespins the assigned color. Then bring the groups back together to practice patterning skills. Hold a long strip of construction paper and invite several students to clip their clothespins to the paper to create a pattern. Ask the children to identify the pattern. Then have volunteers with the correct colored clothespins extend the pattern.

Fold several small rectangles of paper to make tent cards. Label each card with a number, letter, color, or shape. Instruct each child to use only a clothespin to pick up a card. Then ask her to identify the symbol or color on the card she picks up. For added difficulty, have the child pick up and order the letters in her name or in a sight word.

Roll up a large sheet of construction paper; then tape its ends together to form a cylinder. Set the paper cylinder on its end on the floor. Have each child stand over the cylinder and try to drop a clothespin from the tip of his nose into the container. As children become more proficient with this activity, make a cylinder from a smaller piece of construction paper. Ready, aim,…drop!

Get set to race! Put a large supply of clothespins on each table. Call out a number. Have each child connect clothespins together to make a rod of pins matching the number. The child who correctly completes the task first may call out the next number. Add difficulty by giving number sentences or story problems for the children to solve.

Your little ones will be frequent flyers after they try this idea. For each child, cut a 4 1/2" x 6" construction-paper rectangle (one-fourth of a 9" x 12" sheet). Have the child fold and cut the rectangle as shown to make wings. Then instruct her to attach a clothespin to the bottom of her rectangle. To make the paper fly, direct the child to hold the clothespin as high as possible overhead, then release it.

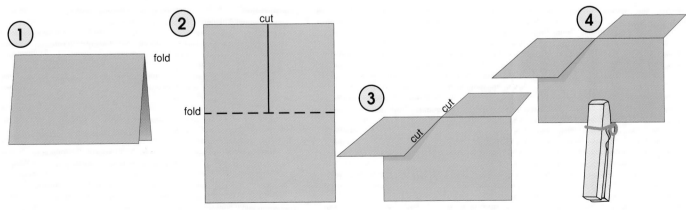

Instant Activities With...
Geoboards

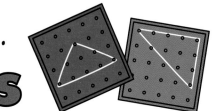

ideas contributed by Carrie Lacher

Give each child a geoboard and several rubber bands. Then read the list of instructions below (or make up other instructions, as desired). Have each child use his bands to follow your directions on his board. When everyone has finished, invite your students to share their creations. Point out that each design is unique, despite having the same components—just like people!

Instructions:
1. Make a straight line.
2. Make a zigzag line.
3. Make two bands cross each other.
4. Make a square.

Play a game of Pass The Board to see what class cooperation can create! Seat your students in a circle and give each child a rubber band. Then place a rubber band on a geoboard and pass the board to the child on your left. Invite her to add her rubber band wherever she desires. Continue passing the board around the circle until it reaches you again. Then show the class the resulting design. What do they think it looks like? Display the design for the children to admire.

Build critical-thinking skills with a round or two of Guess My Shape. To play, give each child in a group a geoboard and several rubber bands. Use a few bands to create a simple geometric shape on your own geoboard, working so that the children cannot see the shape. Then give some clues about your shape. For example, you might say, "My shape has four corners. All its sides are the same." Ask the children to try to figure out what shape you've made and to make the same shape on their own boards. When everyone has made a shape, have the children show their boards. Discuss the variations in the designs that match your shape.

120

 Introduce this activity by asking youngsters to sing "Twinkle, Twinkle, Little Star." Then draw the two star shapes shown below on your chalkboard. Give each of your little ones a geoboard and several rubber bands. Ask each child to choose a star shape and try to copy it onto her geoboard. Line up the finished stars along your chalkboard ledge for a heavenly display!

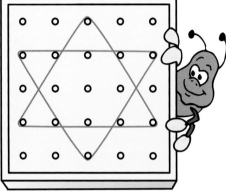

Plink, plink! Rubber bands make beautiful music to little ones' ears! Provide each youngster with a geoboard and several rubber bands in various widths. Encourage children to experiment with stretching the bands over the pegs and plucking them to create a variety of sounds. Finish up by having your geoboard band play along to a favorite musical recording or a class rendition of a favorite song.

Practice sorting by color with your class. Ask the children to sit on the floor. Dump out your collection of rubber bands and ask the children to sort them into piles by color. When all the bands are sorted, divide your class into the same number of groups as you have colors. Have each group take a geoboard and all the bands of its assigned color and create a one-color design. Invite each group to share its finished creation.

This is a pizza. We ordered it, but when the man brought it, a piece was already gone! I think he got hungry!

 Provide each child in a group with a geoboard and a supply of rubber bands. Give the children some time to explore and experiment with creating shapes and figures. Then ask each child to make a picture of something. When everyone is finished, have each child, in turn, share his picture and tell a short story about it.

121

Instant Activities With...
Linking Cubes

ideas contributed by Ada Goren and Angie Kutzer

Direct your little architects to build towers of linking cubes with varying heights. Then have each child trace around several towers on a sheet of paper, lining up the bottoms of the towers along one edge of the paper. Encourage him to use crayons to complete his cityscape.

Encourage little ones to get hooked on measurement by using linking cubes. Have each child make rods of varying lengths, then find classroom objects that match the lengths. Or direct a child to choose an object to measure first, then make a linking-cube rod to match the object's length.

Transform linking cubes into baby birds with this counting rhyme. Give each child five cubes. Have her put one cube on the end of each finger on one hand, then manipulate the cubes to perform the following rhyme. Tweet, tweet!

Five baby birds, ready to soar.
One flies away, so now there are four.
Four baby birds, flapping in the tree.
One flies away, so now there are three.
Three baby birds, learning what to do.
One flies away, so now there are two.
Two baby birds, want to join the fun.
One flies away, so now there is one.
One baby bird, lonely as can be.
Off to find the other birds that left their tree.

Here comes Mama Bird with a tweet, tweet, tweet.
Calls the babies back for a juicy worm treat!
The babies hear their mama, to the tree they fly.
Right back in the nest for lunch—1, 2, 3, 4, 5!

Divide your group into pairs. Have one of the partners in each pair draw a tic-tac-toe grid on a sheet of paper. Invite each pair to play a few rounds of the game using two colors of linking cubes as markers. Here we go, three in a row!

Have each child choose a colored cube without looking in the cube container. When everyone has a cube, instruct students to sort themselves into groups according to the color of their cubes. Then have each group link their cubes together to form a rod. Have a volunteer compare the groups' rods and arrange them in order from shortest to tallest. Complete the activity again and compare the two results.

It's a race to the finish with this number-recognition game. Set out a supply of separated linking cubes on each table. Call out a number from one to ten. Challenge each student to link cubes together to form a rod that matches the number as quickly as possible. Have the child hold her rod in the air when she finishes. For added difficulty, give simple addition or subtraction sentences to solve. Who's the fastest thinker and linker in your class?

Construct a quick and easy graph—using two colors of linking cubes—in order to tally a classroom vote. Ask a question such as "Do you like to play basketball?" Designate one color to represent "yes" and a different color to represent "no." Invite each child to respond to the question by choosing the appropriately colored cube and adding it to the yes or no tower. What's the verdict?

Instant Activities With...
ANIMAL FIGURES

ideas contributed by Angie Kutzer and Linda Ludlow

Put all of your animal figures in one container. Designate one animal as the "winner." Then have each child pick a figure from the container without looking. The child who picks the designated animal may name the winning animal for the next round.

Add a twist to the traditional song "Old MacDonald" by using your whole collection of animal figures. Ask a volunteer to choose one animal from the collection. Discuss where the animal lives and what sound or movement it makes. To modify the verse below, substitute the habitat, the beginning consonant sound of the habitat, the animal's name, and the animal's sound or movement. Then sing the verse and journey on down to the farm, or desert, or sea!

(sung to the tune of "Old MacDonald")

Took a trip down to the [sea].
[S]E-[S]I-[S]E-[S]I-[S]O
And in the [sea] we saw a [shark].
[S]E-[S]I-[S]E-[S]I-[S]O
With a [chomp, chomp] here and a [chomp, chomp] there,
Here a [chomp], there a [chomp], everywhere a [chomp, chomp].
Took a trip down to the [sea].
[S]E-[S]I-[S]E-[S]I-[S]O

Discuss with your students how many animals use camouflage as a defense. Instruct each child to choose an animal figure from your collection. Then direct him to use a sheet of paper and crayons to make a camouflaged background that will hide and protect his animal.

Kevin

124

Use five of your animal figures to give little ones practice with ordinal numbers. Place the figures in a line; then question students on which figures are first, second, third, and so on. Invite a volunteer to rearrange the lineup; then ask questions such as "Where is the elephant? Where is the gorilla? Is the whale first or fourth?" For another variation, give each figure to a different child. Call out a lineup and have the children place their figures in the correct positions.

Display several animal figures on a tabletop. Have students close their eyes while you remove a figure from the display. Then invite volunteers to guess which animal is missing. Have the child who guesses correctly remove an animal in the next round of this guessing game.

Sorting, sorting, sorting! Choose some of the suggestions shown here to keep little minds busy thinking and categorizing animal figures. Then challenge students to come up with some of their own groupings.

- size
- color
- body coverings
- habitats

- plant/meat eaters
- wild/tame
- number of legs
- parents/babies

OO-OO-OO!

Seat your students in a circle. Have students pass a container of animal figures around the circle as they chant the following rhyme. At the end of the rhyme, encourage the child holding the container to pull out an animal figure and dramatize its movements.

Animals, animals, 1,2,3;
Show us what animal you'd like to be!

125

Instant Activities With...
PASTA

ideas contributed by Jan Brennan and Mackie Rhodes

Cook up some creative storytelling "pasta-bilities" with this idea! Put some pasta in a large container to represent a pot of pasta. Use a spoon or a similar object to stir the pasta while reciting this rhyme; then say a sentence to begin a story. Repeat the procedure, inviting each child in turn to stir the pasta and then to add a sentence to the story. If desired, record the story on a sheet of chart paper.

> Stir it up once, nice and hot.
> Stir up a story in our pasta pot!

Here's a counting chant that youngsters will find "pasta-tively" delightful. To begin, give each child ten pieces of pasta. Ask students to count out their pasta to the words in this chant.

> One pasta, two pasta, three pasta, four;
> Five pasta, six pasta, seven pasta, more!
> Eight pasta, nine pasta, ten pasta, too.
> I like counting my pasta with you!

These instant instruments will be a big hit with youngsters. Give each child a few pieces of pasta. Have him cup his hands together so that the pasta moves freely—but does not fall out—when he shakes his hands. Using pasta pieces cupped between your own hands, demonstrate a simple rhythmic pattern; then invite youngsters to repeat the pattern. Increase the challenge by having students repeat a pattern paired with a different hands position, such as above their heads, to their left sides, or between their knees.

A handful of pasta can go a long way in helping youngsters share information about themselves. Ask each child to create a glued pasta design to represent something about herself, such as her name, pet, or favorite food. Then invite each child in turn to tell about her design. That's pasta with personality!

126

Use this peekaboo pasta activity for practicing visual-memory skills. Pair students; then give each partner in a pair an identical set of five to eight pasta pieces. Have each partner place her pasta pieces on a table. Ask one child in the pair to cover her pasta with a sheet of paper and then remove one, two, or three pasta pieces from under the paper—without revealing these pieces to her partner. Have her uncover the remaining pasta, then challenge her partner to compare the two sets to determine which pieces were removed.

If you're in a sticky situation with time to fill, these pasta trains will get you back on track. To make a train, give each child a length of tape and some pasta; then have him arrange the pasta pieces in a simple pattern on the sticky side of the tape. Invite youngsters to move their trains to this rhyme. Each time the rhyme is repeated, use either the word *left* or *right* for the underlined word. Chug-a-chug-a-chug!

> Pasta train chugging down the track;
> Rolling to the [right] with a clickety-clack.
> Out comes a steam-puff from its stack;
> Time to turn around and head on back!

Challenge youngsters to build as many different designs and structures as possible using only one type of pasta. (For instance, a child might use wagon-wheel pasta to create a pyramid, a house, a flower, and a tree.) Then invite students to construct additional designs using two types of pasta in combination. Get those gears moving—it's construction time!

This paired pasta activity will have youngsters seeing double! Divide your class into pairs; then give identical sets of pasta to the partners in each pair. (For example, you could give each child three macaroni noodles, two wagon wheels, and one shell pasta.) Ask one child in each pair to create a design with his pasta. Have his partner reproduce that design with his own pasta. Then invite the partners to switch roles so that each child has the opportunity to both create and reproduce a pasta design. Double the pasta—double the fun!

Instant Activities With...

BALLS

ideas contributed by Joyce Montag

Place a class supply of chairs in a circle, about six inches apart. Have each student take a seat. Tell students that the object of this game is to pass the ball around the circle *without* getting out of their chairs (although they may sit on the edges of their seats). Give one child a ball and ask him to pass it to the child on his right. If the ball makes it successfully all the way around the circle, increase the difficulty of the game. Ask each child to bounce the ball to the child next to him, or to pass the ball using only one hand.

Little ones will get a kick out of this game! Have children sit on the floor, forming a circle. Show them how to place their feet flat on the floor in front of them with knees bent and hands palm side down on the floor beside their hips. Explain that the one rule for this game is that the ball can be moved only with feet, not hands. Encourage the children to try to keep the ball within the circle. If the ball rolls outside the circle, it must be retrieved with feet, not hands. Begin the game by kicking the ball to someone on the other side of the circle and let the fun begin.

This activity is best for a blacktop or sidewalk area. Supply each child with a ball. Explain that each child is going to bounce her ball until she hears a given signal (such as a toot on a whistle). When she hears the signal, each child should stop bouncing, place her ball on the ground, and run to find a different ball. Continue the activity until interest wanes.

Balls aren't just for gross-motor fun, of course. How about an art activity? Ask each child to choose a partner. Supply each pair with a ball, a pair of scissors, and a generous strip of masking tape. Invite the pairs to use pieces of tape to add facial features to their balls. Encourage each pair to share its finished face with the class.

Use two lines of masking tape on your floor or two chalk lines on a sidewalk to lay out a curving path about two feet wide. Then invite each child to guide a ball along the path, using only his feet to steer the ball. As a variation, provide a ruler and have each child steer the ball along the path using only the ruler.

 Bounce your way into numeral recognition! On a sidewalk or blacktop area, use chalk to draw ten circles. Label each circle randomly with the numerals one through ten. Invite one child at a time to bounce the ball in each circle, beginning with number one and finishing with number ten. Vary the activity by drawing a circle for each alphabet letter, and having youngsters bounce their way through the ABCs!

 Use a playground ball to practice ordinal numbers. Use chalk to draw a line of five circles on a sidewalk or blacktop area. Have your students line up at one end of the line of circles. Give a ball to the first child and give a command, such as "Bounce the ball in the [third] circle." Continue with the other children, changing the ordinal number as each child takes his turn.

 Gather all the balls you have handy in your classroom. Ask students to sort them by size, color, or type. Then ask students to brainstorm a list of all the kinds of balls they can think of. Beach balls, footballs, baseballs, tennis balls, soccer balls…this could be a long list!

Instant Activities With...
WOODEN BLOCKS

ideas contributed by Linda Gordetsky and Angie Kutzer

Challenge students to work cooperatively to build a tower using as many blocks as possible. Have each child take a turn adding one block until the tower falls. Count aloud the number of blocks used in the tower; then encourage students to increase the number of blocks used in their next tower.

Use your supply of wooden blocks to give little ones some practice in patterning. Give each child two blocks and keep two for yourself. With your blocks, tap a rhythmic pattern for children to copy. Continue in this manner until volunteers are ready to create patterns of their own for others to repeat. It's toe-tappin', finger-snappin', block-clappin' fun!

Pair up your students for some block writing. Have partners work together to form letters with blocks. Encourage older children to spell each other's names and basic sight words.

Your little ones will be in great shape when they trace the geometrical outlines of blocks. Give each child two different-shaped blocks. Direct him to trace the outline of one of the blocks on a sheet of paper several times in different places and turned different ways. Then instruct him to follow the same procedure with the other block, overlapping shapes for an interesting effect. Encourage the child to finish this shapely work of art by using a different colored crayon to color each outline. Blocks and art? You bet!

Katie

Give each child a block. Write her initials on a piece of tape and attach it to the block. Have her slide her block from one end of a table to the other. See which child can slide her block closest to the edge of the table without having it fall off or be knocked off by someone else's block.

Have students sort your supply of blocks by size and shape. Then count the blocks in each group to find out which has the most, the fewest, or the same number of blocks.

Outline an area on the floor with tape or on the sidewalk with chalk. Direct students to use blocks to cover as much of the area as possible. Count how many blocks it took to fill in the outline.

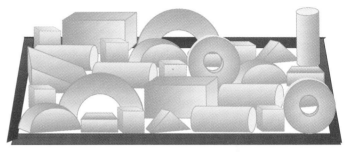

Seat a pair of students across from each other. Give each child five blocks identical to his partner's. Have one child close his eyes while his partner builds a structure with her five blocks. Direct the first child to open his eyes and study the formation for a few seconds. Then have the builder hide her structure behind a sheet of construction paper so that it is no longer visible to her partner. Challenge the partner to use his memory to build an identical structure. Compare the resulting formation to the original; then have the partners switch jobs.

Instant Activities With...
MAGNETIC
LETTERS AND NUMBERS

ideas contributed by Diane Gilliam and Ada Goren

ABC Incorporate some movement into your study of letters and numbers with this fun activity. Have a youngster select a magnetic letter or number from your collection. Then have her select two or three classmates and direct them on how to cooperatively form the letter with their bodies.

123 Your little detectives will be eager to crack the case of the mystery letter or number. Secretly place one magnetic letter or number in a paper bag or a box. Invite a child to reach into the container and attempt to identify the letter or number by feeling it. Once the case is solved, encourage all your detectives to write the letter or number in the air with their mystery writing sticks. Then give another youngster an opportunity to solve a new mystery!

ABC Remind your youngsters that all letters are formed in one of three ways: with lines, with curves, or with lines *and* curves. Write a few letters on your chalkboard or point them out on your alphabet display to make your explanation clear. Then give the children a collection of magnetic letters and ask them to sort the letters into the three groups of letter formations.

123 Use magnetic letters and numbers to practice estimation skills. Fill a small see-through container (such as a baby-food jar) with magnetic letters and numbers. Give each child a chance to examine the container and guess how many magnetic letters and numbers might be inside. Then cooperatively count the container's contents and see whose guess was closest to the actual number.

ABC Send your students on an alphabet scavenger hunt to help them practice beginning sounds. Select a few magnetic letters with which your students are familiar. Then divide your class into teams and give each team a letter. Ask the children to explore the classroom and find as many objects as possible that have their assigned letter's beginning sound. Have all the groups gather in your group area to show their finds.

123 Collect six magnetic letters and place them on a tray. Ask a small group of students to look closely and try to remember the letters they see. Then remove the tray from the children's sight and remove two or three of the letters. Bring out the tray and ask the children to tell you which letters are missing. As an extension, ask youngsters to name words that begin with each letter on the tray.

ABC Give youngsters practice with matching numerals and sets. Draw several sets of simple objects on a magnetic chalkboard. For example, you might draw two hearts, five happy faces, and seven flowers. Then ask volunteers to come to the board and stick the corresponding magnetic numeral beside each set.

If your chalkboard isn't magnetic, draw the sets of objects on sheets of paper. Lay the papers on a tabletop and simply have children place the corresponding magnetic numeral on each sheet.

123 Display your magnetic letters vertically on your chalkboard in alphabetical order. Select a brainstorming topic—such as names, foods, toys, animals, or things found at the circus. Invite your youngsters to call out as many items as they can think of that fit the category as you fill in the alphabet chart. Can they think of an item for every letter?

ABC   Pass around magnetic numbers for some counting practice with movement mixed in. Place all your magnetic numbers in a container. Have the children sit in a circle and pass the container from child to child as you play some lively music. Stop the music and ask the youngster holding the container to draw out a number. Ask her to identify the number, but not to tell her classmates. Then invite her to stand and perform a movement of her choice—such as jumping jacks or hops—a corresponding number of times. Have the other children count her movements, then identify the number she drew.

123   On a magnetic chalkboard or file cabinet, place a series of letters or numbers. Leave out a letter or number in the sequence. Then ask volunteers to determine which letter or numeral is missing. If youngsters find this a challenge, encourage them to refer to your classroom alphabet and number displays for help.

ABC   Select a word family you wish to review with your older students. Working on a magnetic surface, place the magnetic letters that spell a word from that family on the surface. Scatter some extra letters at the edge of the surface, some of which can be used to make other words in the word family and some of which can't. Invite volunteers to take turns substituting letters to create new words in the word family. Be sure to explore the idea that some letters won't form real words, but will make nonsense words.

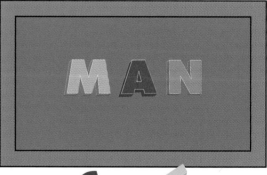

123   This name game is guaranteed to produce the giggles! Use magnetic letters to spell a child's name on a magnetic surface. Then substitute different beginning letters and invite youngsters to pronounce the results. Continue with as many classmates' names as time permits.

134

ABC Distribute the magnetic numerals necessary to form the numbers one through ten to a group of ten students. Then ask the children to place their numbers in order *backwards* on a magnetic surface or a tabletop. Once the numbers are in order, count down from ten to one and invite your little ones to join you in an imaginary rocket-ship trip around the classroom. 3, 2, 1…blast off!

123 Invite a small group of children to try this letter-matching activity. Divide your collection of magnetic letters evenly among a group of students. Then invite one child to find a printed word that she recognizes somewhere in your classroom—a nametag, a word from a pocket chart, or even the color word on a crayon. Have her bring the word to the group. Then ask the children to match their letters to the letters in the word to co-operatively copy it. Then give another child a turn to hunt for a word to copy.

ABC Build students' self-esteem with this variation on a tried-and-true activity. Use magnetic letters to spell a child's name vertically on a magnetic chalkboard. Then ask the child's classmates to supply descriptive words or phrases about him. Use chalk to fill in some of the words around the magnetic letters, creating an acrostic. Discuss where each magnetic letter falls in the description—at the beginning, in the middle, or at the end. Review all the glowing compliments before going on to another child's name.

Cotton Balls And Cotton Swabs

ideas contributed by Angie Kutzer and Suzanne Moore

Distribute seven cotton swabs to each child. Demonstrate how to curve a swab by gently bending it so that the cotton tips touch. (The tips will spring back, but the swab will retain a curved shape.) Then have each child bend three of his swabs. Show students how to form letters with the curved and straight swabs; then encourage them to make some letters on their own. As an extension, have students work together to form every letter of the alphabet and glue each formation onto a long strip of bulletin-board paper.

Little ones will enjoy creating patterns with cotton swabs. Give each child a handful of swabs. Call out patterns such as "tall, long, tall, long" and "up, up, down, down" and have each child form and extend the patterns. Then encourage students to come up with some of their own patterns for classmates to extend.

Have students line up, one behind another, at a designated line. Give each child a cotton ball. Direct the first child to throw her cotton ball as far as she can. Mark the distance with a piece of tape labeled with her initials. Continue in this manner until everyone gets a turn. Then have students gather around the throwing area to compare the results.

This tabletop activity will help little ones' eye-hand coordination. Make a target by drawing a circle on a sheet of construction paper. Place the target in the center of the table. Give each child a cotton ball and a cotton swab. (Pencils can substitute for swabs.) Have each child take a turn "putting" her cotton ball from the edge of the table toward the target. Direct the rest of the group to count aloud the number of strokes it takes to get the ball in the target. Any holes-in-one?

Reinforce the concepts of *greater than* and *less than* by using cotton balls and cotton swabs. Give each child a small handful of each object. Direct her to match one cotton ball to one swab and continue using one-to-one correspondence until one group has leftovers. Then ask the child which group has more or less. Challenge her to add or take away cotton balls or swabs so that both groups have the same number of items.

What's the weather? A gray and gloomy day is forecast for this art activity. Give each child a sheet of white paper and two cotton balls. Have him use the side of a pencil tip to lightly shade in the entire sheet. Then direct him to rub the cotton balls over the shading to blend and smear the pencil marks. To make storm clouds, ask each child to turn his cotton balls over, gently pull them apart, and glue them to the top of his paper. Then encourage him to use crayons to complete his rainy-day picture with a soggy scene. If time permits, finish the activity with a reading of a favorite rain story.

Use a cotton ball to develop vocabulary, work on comparisons, and discuss the concept of weight. Give each student a cotton ball. Encourage discussion as he compares the weight of his cotton ball in one hand to other classroom objects in his other hand. Distribute a sheet of paper to each child. Have him glue his cotton ball to the paper; then have him draw one of the heavier objects that he found beside the cotton ball. Bind the students' drawings together along with a cover sheet titled "A Cotton Ball Is Lighter Than…" to create a book for your reading center.

Give each child a cotton swab and a cup of water. Invite him to use a lapboard or the classroom chalkboard to practice letter and number formations. Can he write his whole name before the water evaporates?

137

Instant Activities With...
STICKY DOTS

ideas contributed by Angie Kutzer and Suzanne Moore

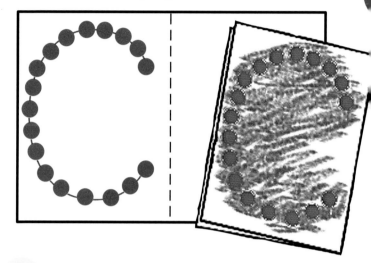

Give each child a sheet of duplicating paper and some sticky dots. Instruct her to fold her paper in half, then unfold it. On one half of her paper, have her use a pencil to draw a shape, numeral, or letter and then cover its outline with dots. Direct her to fold the paper again, with the blank half covering the dots. Then have her use the side of an unwrapped crayon to make a rubbing of her sticky-dot figure. Cut the paper halves apart and mount them onto construction paper. Your young artists will be seeing double!

Create an instant graph with a large sheet of construction paper and sticky dots. Write a question—such as "Do you like green peas?"—across the top of the paper; then draw a line dividing the paper into two sections. Label one section "yes" and the other section "no." Invite each child to respond by putting a sticky dot in the row of her choice. Count the responses and discuss the results.

Put sticky dots on each child's right hand and foot. Play a quick game of Simon Says, or sing "The Hokey-Pokey" to practice the concepts of *right* and *left*. "That's what it's all about!"

Reinforce numerical order as your little ones create their own dot-to-dot pictures. Demonstrate how to stick dots on a sheet of paper to create a simple geometric shape. Label each dot with a different sequential numeral; then connect the dots with a marker. Give each child some dots and a sheet of paper. Help him create his own dot-to-dot picture using a shape of his choice. More advanced youngsters will enjoy creating dot-to-dots for their classmates to complete.

Stick to the basic skills of counting, spatial relationships, and listening with this dot activity. Give each child a sheet of paper and several sticky dots. Instruct students to listen carefully to your instructions telling where to place the dots (sample instructions are shown here). To add more difficulty, use multicolored dots and include a specific color in each direction.

Directions:
Put one dot in the middle of your paper.
Place three dots at the bottom of your paper.
Put one dot in each corner.
Line up all of your blue dots across the top of your page.
Put two green dots on each side of your page.

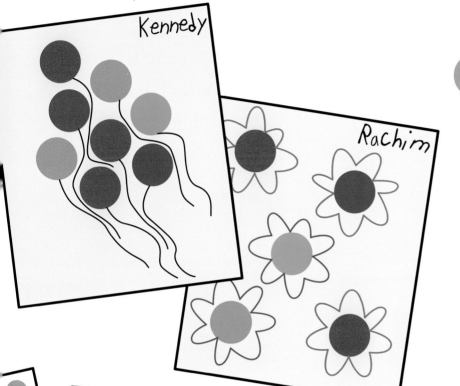

Reinforce one-to-one correspondence by using sticky dots and paper. Have each child turn his dots into balloons or flowers by sticking them onto his paper and using a crayon to add a string or petals to each one. For more advanced practice, give each child an equal number of two colors of sticky dots. Have him line up all the dots of one color on one side of the page and all the dots of the other color on the opposite side of the page. Instruct him to draw lines between the dots, giving each dot a different-colored partner.

Give each child the same two colors or sizes of sticky dots and some paper strips. Encourage her to create a pattern with some of her dots on one of the strips. Then have her trade strips with a classmate. Instruct her to look at her classmate's pattern and copy it on another paper strip. If time permits, have the child trade strips again with someone new.

Use sticky dots to make instant finger puppets. Give each child ten sticky dots. Have her draw a happy face on each dot, then stick each dot to a different fingertip. Sing several favorite counting songs and rhymes, such as "Ten Little Indians" and "Five Little Ducks," to get those little fingers wiggling.

Instant Activities With...
TEDDY-BEAR COUNTERS

ideas contributed by Angie Kutzer and Vicki Pacchetti

Pull out the teddy-bear counters, and invite your little ones to brush up on counting and one-to-one correspondence. Have each child arrange ten bears into a straight line. Then ask him to echo you in chanting each line of the following military rhyme while he points to each bear:

Here are ten bears in a line:
Standing tall and looking fine.
One bear, two bears, three bears, four;
Five bears, six bears, seven bears, more;
Eight bears, nine bears, then there's ten.
Start at one and count again.
Sound off.   *(teacher)*
1, 2.   *(students)*
Sound off.   *(teacher)*
3, 4.   *(students)*
Break it on down.   *(teacher)*
5, 6, 7, 8, 9, 10...**The End!**   *(students)*

Build your students' visual memory with this small-group activity. Give each child one bear of each color. Arrange three of your own bear counters into a row. Have one youngster study your lineup, copy the arrangement with his counters, and then close his eyes. Remove one of your bears, rearrange your bears' order, or do nothing to your lineup. Then invite the child to open his eyes and compare his lineup to yours to decide if the two are the same or different. Encourage him to use his own bear counters to explain anything that is different or to hold up the bear that is missing. Continue the activity with the other children in the group.

Divide your class into pairs. Have one partner in each pair draw a tic-tac-toe grid on a sheet of paper. Direct each child to get five same-colored teddy-bear counters that are a different color from her partner's bears. It's time to play Tic-Tac-Teddy!

Encourage your little cubs to use their imaginations and problem-solving skills. Provide each youngster with enough teddy-bear counters to use in acting out simple story problems. Ask volunteers to help you create bear-related scenarios that require addition, subtraction, or other readiness skills. Use the following samples to get you started:

Three bears were slurping on a honeycomb.
Two more bears joined them.
How many bears are eating now?

Six bears went down to the river.
Four bears decided to take a swim.
How many bears stayed dry?

Brown Bear has two brothers.
Brown Bear has one sister.
How many cubs are in Brown Bear's family?

One mother bear hibernated all winter.
Seven bears came out of her cave in spring.
How many cubs did the mother bear have?

 Give each child a bear counter of each color and size. Challenge each youngster to form a line with his counters by following your oral directions. Call out directions using the colors and sizes of the counters, as well as ordinal numbers, such as "Put a small yellow bear first." Repeat the directions so that each child can check his accuracy.

 Provide each child or small group of children with ten bear counters. Invite the class to sing the traditional song "Ten In A Bed" and act out the song with their counters. If time allows, adapt the song to include different locations such as the version shown here.

There were ten by the pool,
And the little one said, "I'm hot; I'm hot!"
So they all moved closer and one jumped in.

Continue counting down from nine through two, and finish with:
There was one by the pool,
And that little bear said, "I'm hot; I'm hot!"
So he moved closer and then jumped in.
Ker-splash!

Instant Activities With...
Housekeeping Dishes

ideas contributed by Rachel Castro and Angie Kutzer

Give each child a plastic fork and a plastic spoon from your housekeeping center. Call out the name of a food. Have the child hold up the utensil used to eat the food. Add a little more difficulty by also naming foods that can be eaten with your hands. Some examples are shown here. Bon appétit!

Fork	Spoon	Hands
spaghetti	ice cream	hamburger
salad	cereal	pizza
broccoli	soup	sandwich
meat	gelatin	chips
pancakes	pudding	corn on the cob

Set students up for a quick review of positional words. Distribute a cup, a plate, utensils, and a large sheet of construction paper to each child. Have him set his place at the table by listening and following your directions. Give one direction at a time and encourage him to position the appropriate piece in the appropriate place. Be sure to emphasize words such as *middle, above, below, beside, left,* and *right.* For less confusion, have students bend the right corners of their placemats before you begin.

After learning how to properly arrange a table setting, youngsters will be in a hurry to set the table during this game. Gather the plates, cups, and utensils from your dramatic-play center. Into separate paper bags insert two of each item, so that each bag contains two plates, two cups, two forks, two knives, and two spoons. Divide your class into as many groups as you have bags. Position each of the bags the same short distance from each team. Place a large sheet of construction paper beside each bag. To play the game, a member from each team runs to his team's bag and without looking, pulls an object from the bag. If the object is needed for his team's table setting, he puts it in its proper place. If the object has already been picked, he puts it back in the bag and runs back to his team. Play continues until all of the teams complete their table settings.

It's orange.
It's a vegetable.
Rabbits eat it.

Serve students extra helpings of clues and watch them fill up with guesses for this mystery-food game. Seat youngsters in a circle. Give a child a plastic plate and a series of clues describing a mystery food. For example, you might say, "It's orange. It's a vegetable. Rabbits eat it." Encourage the child holding the plate to guess the name of the food. Give more clues if necessary. Once the child guesses correctly, have her pass the plate to the next child for the next set of clues. Continue until each child has had a turn.

Collect matching pairs of several plastic cooking utensils, dishes, and pots—such as two spoons, two cups, and two frying pans. Ask several volunteers to stand in front of the group. Give each volunteer a different plastic piece to hold behind his back so that it cannot be seen. The remaining students then take turns guessing which two volunteers are holding each matching pair of objects. As two volunteers' names are called, they show the objects they're holding. If the objects match, the two volunteers sit down. When all of the matches have been found, redistribute the objects to new volunteers for another round of memory fun.

This letter-association game is sure to tempt tummies and tickle tastebuds. Seat your students in a circle. Bring a plate, a bowl, and a cup to the circle. Show youngsters each of the dishes. Discuss the name of each dish, its beginning letter, and other words that begin with that letter. Then pass one of the objects around the circle and encourage each child to use the corresponding sentence pattern shown here to create a silly sentence. Continue in this manner for each dish.

Please pass a plate of [peas].
Bring back a bowl of [berries].
Could you carry a cup of [corn]?

143

ideas contributed by Ada Goren, Angie Kutzer, and Mackie Rhodes

My cookie is a school bus and it's going on a field trip!

Put a new twist on a cookie snack by asking youngsters to use their imaginations before they eat. Have each child imagine that his cookie is a vehicle. Invite each child, in turn, to tell what kind of vehicle he imagines his cookie to be and to where it is traveling. Then encourage each youngster to imagine his mouth as the vehicle's destination. Yum! Those cookie vehicles are tasty!

Practice higher-level math when you challenge a small group of youngsters to divide a supply of cookies. To each small group, distribute a number of cookies, and ask the children in the group to divide the cookies fairly. Make this activity more interesting for older children by giving them a number of cookies that doesn't divide evenly. Discuss their solutions for what to do with the extra cookie or cookies.

Cook up a little poetry during snacktime! Give each child a cookie; then teach youngsters the poem below. Invite them to stop to take bites and chew at the appropriate points in the poem.

Gonna eat my cookie—looks yummy all right!
Here I go; I'll take a bite.   *(bite)*
Just chomp right down and chew, chew, chew.
Now I'll take bite number two.   *(bite)*
This cookie is tasty as tasty can be!
I'm ready to take bite number three.   *(bite)*
I'm crunchin' and munchin'. Is there any more?
Open my mouth—bite number four.   *(bite)*
You're almost gone, my sweet cookie friend;
One last bite and that's the end!   *(bite)*

144

Cookies LOOK	Cookies TASTE	Cookies FEEL	Cookies SMELL	Cookies SOUND
round	good	crumbly	good	crunchy
brown with black spots	sweet	bumpy		quiet
black with curvy edges				

Focus on the five senses with this cookie-eating activity. Give each child one or two cookies to eat. Ask the children to think about how their cookies *look, taste, feel, smell,* and *sound* as they are eating. As the students eat, make a chart similar to the one shown on your chalkboard or a sheet of chart paper. Then ask youngsters to list descriptive words and phrases to add under each heading.

This activity will be music to your youngsters' ears—and mouths! Before you teach your students the chant below, distribute two cookies to each child. Then demonstrate how to tap two cookies together gently to create sounds. (Provide extra cookies in case some get broken.) Instruct the children to follow your tapping pattern at the appropriate point in the chant. Then invite all the players of cookie music to munch those makeshift instruments!

Cookies, cookies can't be beat
When you crave a crunchy, musical treat!
Tap two together to make this sound:
(Teacher taps a pattern, and children copy it.)
The tastiest music anywhere around!

Ask each youngster to estimate the number of cookies in a jar, bag, or box. Then count together to determine the actual number. Allow the child whose guess was closest to the actual number to pass out a cookie snack to her classmates.

After a cookie snack, ask your little ones to put on their thinking caps! Encourage your children to brainstorm as many kinds of cookies as they can as you record the list on your chalkboard or a sheet of chart paper. Then take a vote to determine the class's favorite cookie, and tally the results. If desired, draw a simple bar graph on the board or paper, and graph the results of your vote.

145

Instant Activities With...
Paper And Tape

ideas contributed by Ada Goren, Angie Kutzer, and Mackie Rhodes

Give little ones an opportunity to work on eye-hand coordination with a simple-to-make game of toss. Have each youngster roll a sheet of construction paper into a cone shape and tape it in place. Then have each child choose a partner. Provide each pair with another half-sheet of paper to wad into a paper ball. Encourage the partners to toss the paper ball back and forth, using their paper cones to throw and catch.

Little ones love to give drawings to their moms and dads. Use paper and tape to create some special child-made envelopes for carrying these important messages of love. Show youngsters how to fold up one short edge of a sheet of paper, then tape the sides closed. Complete the envelope by folding down the top flap and sealing it shut with a bit of tape. Then assist each child in making her own envelope. When the envelopes are complete—or later in the day—give youngsters time to draw some special pictures, fold them up, and slip them inside the envelopes to take home.

Look out! Here's an activity your youngsters will love! Supply each child with a sheet of paper and a length of tape. Show her how to roll the paper into a tube and tape it in place. Then play a traditional game of I Spy. Invite each child to look through her tube and silently choose an object in the room. Encourage her to give a few clues to help her classmates locate the object. The child who guesses correctly may "spy" the next object.

If desired, vary the activity so that each child makes two paper tubes, then tapes them together to resemble binoculars.

Begin a fashion trend among your preschoolers or kindergartners—paper jewelry! Set out paper strips and tape, and encourage little ones to fashion bracelets and rings. If desired, invite the children to wear their creations for a jewelry fashion show!

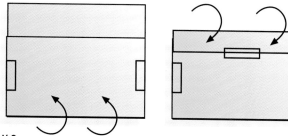

Give your students' visual-discrimination skills a workout with these torn-paper puzzles. Have each youngster tear a sheet of construction paper into a few large pieces. Then have each child choose a partner and switch sets of paper pieces. Ask each child to reassemble his partner's paper and tape the pieces back into place.

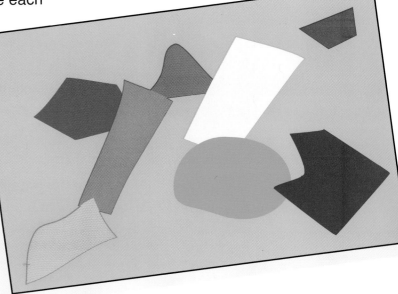

Create a class cooperative collage of color! To prepare, tape a large piece of bulletin-board paper to a wall within children's reach. Set out your construction-paper scrap box and ask each youngster to choose a piece of paper. Place a rolled piece of tape on each child's scrap. Then have each child, in turn, close his eyes and stick his scrap of paper to the larger paper. When everyone has applied his scrap paper, observe the results. Beautiful!

Little ones will practice patterning and fine-motor skills when they construct paper chains. Set out tape and a supply of construction-paper strips in a variety of colors. Demonstrate how to roll a strip into a link and tape it in place. Also show youngsters how to thread another strip of paper through the completed link and tape it in place, beginning a linked chain. Then invite each child to choose two or three colors of strips and create his own chain in a repeating pattern. Encourage each youngster to explain his pattern to the other children at his table.

Let imaginations take flight with this activity! Give each child two sheets of construction paper. Instruct each student to tear strips resembling fringe along one long edge of his papers. Then tape each child's fringed papers to his sleeves to create imaginary wings. Ask each child to imagine he is a winged creature. What is he? How does he move? Where is he flying? Give each child a chance to tell about and dramatize his animal.

147

Instant Activities With...

ideas contributed by Rachel Castro

Little ones love the opportunity to write on the chalkboard—so they'll be eager to try this activity that provides practice in letter recognition and name writing. Write a letter of the alphabet on your chalkboard. Then teach youngsters the song below. Any student who has the letter in her name may then come to the chalkboard to write her name. Ask her to show you where the letter is located in her name.

(sung to the tune of "The Farmer In The Dell")

What letter do you see?
What letter do you see?
Is it a letter in your name?
What letter do you see?

If you have an ample supply of individual chalkboards, try this sequencing activity. Ask each of ten children to write a different numeral from one to ten on her chalkboard. Then challenge the children to hold their chalkboards and place themselves in numerical order. If you have a class supply of individual boards, try sequencing the alphabet.

Storytelling will take off with this cooperative class idea. Begin by drawing an object on your chalkboard. Begin a story about the object. Then hand the chalk to one of your youngsters and ask her to continue the story and add to your drawing. Continue until all the children have had a turn to add to the story and illustration.

And there were apples on the tree...

Older kindergartners will enjoy this simple spelling activity. Distribute chalk and individual chalkboards to several children. Ask each child to write a specific letter on his board. Then call out three letters from a simple word, such as *cat,* in random order. Have the three children holding those letters come to the front of the group. Then give the rest of the class a clue about the word you have in mind, such as "This is a pet." Ask for a volunteer to put the children—and letters—in order to form the word. Continue with other words, giving every child an opportunity to be a part of a word.

Use chalk and individual chalkboards to check up on students' counting abilities. Distribute chalk and a chalkboard to each child in your group. Then draw a set of simple pictures on your class chalkboard, such as hearts, circles, or stars. Ask the children to count the pictures and write the corresponding numeral on their boards. To check, simply have the students hold up their chalkboards for you to see.

For an artistic activity, give each child an individual chalkboard and a piece of chalk. Then draw two shapes on your chalkboard for the children to see. Ask your students to copy the two shapes onto their individual boards, placing the shapes wherever they desire. Then encourage each of your young artists to draw in the details to turn the two shapes into a picture.

Gather eight individual chalkboards. On each board draw a simple shape, so that you have two circles, two triangles, two squares, and two rectangles. Then ask eight children to stand in front of the class. Hand each child a board, but ask him to keep it turned so that the shape is hidden from the group. Ask a volunteer to name two of the standing children, who then flip their boards over to reveal their shapes. If the shapes match, take the boards and have those children sit down. Give the student who found the match a turn to hold a chalkboard in the next round. If the shapes don't match, have the children flip the boards back over and give someone else a turn to find a match.

Instant Activities With...
Sticky Notes

ideas contributed by Vicki Pacchetti

Invite your little ones to crack the case of "The Secret Sticky Note." On a class supply of sticky notes, draw a variety of shapes, letters, numbers, or color swatches. Without showing the note to the child, stick a different note on each child's back. Then have each youngster pick a partner. Have each child's partner give him clues as to what is on his mystery sticky note. Once the child guesses, have the partners switch roles so the other child can guess.

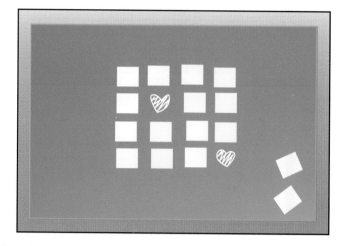

You have that many arms.

Play a traditional game of Concentration with a sticky-note twist. Quickly draw several pairs of objects on your chalkboard or a sheet of chart paper. Draw the objects in rows, evenly spaced, and without placing the two objects in each pair next to one another. Then cover each picture with a sticky note. Once the gameboard is complete, invite little ones to join you. Have a volunteer peel off two sticky notes to reveal the drawings beneath. If the drawings match, the child may keep the sticky notes. If the drawings do not match, have him replace the covers and let another child have a turn. Continue until all the pairs are revealed.

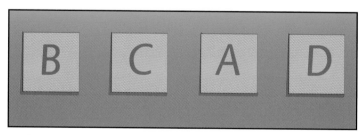

Here's a quick way to review the sequence of numbers or letters. Write each number or letter in a sequence on a separate sticky note. Stick the notes in random order to your chalkboard. Then ask a volunteer to put the numbers or letters in the proper order.

A pad of sticky notes will make graphing a snap! Decide on a question and print it on your chalkboard or a sheet of chart paper. Label the rows or columns of your graph with possible responses. Then distribute a sticky note to each child. Invite each child to write her name on her note. Then have each youngster in turn come up to the graph and place her note in the desired row or column. Discuss the results of the class graph.

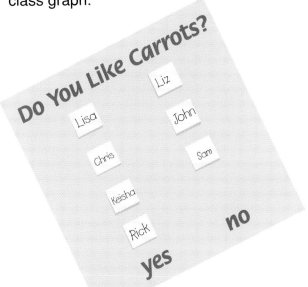

Fill a few extra moments by passing out praise! Grab a pad of sticky notes and a marker. Sketch a simple happy face on the top note. Present this official Sticky-Note Smile to one of your students, mentioning something wonderful about his work or behavior that makes him deserving. Continue with Sticky-Note Smiles and good words all around!

Use a supply of 3" x 5" sticky notes to make this lift-the-flap class book. Give each child a sheet of paper, crayons, and a large sticky note. Explain that you are going to create a class book titled "What's Under The Bed?" Ask each youngster to affix her sticky note to the center of her paper and color it to resemble a blanket or quilt. Have her add details, such as a headboard or bedposts, to complete the look of a bed. Then have her lift up the sticky note and illustrate an object in the area under the note. If time permits, write each child's dictation about her object below her drawing. Then bind all the pages together with a cover bearing the book title. Share the book with the class before adding it to your class library.

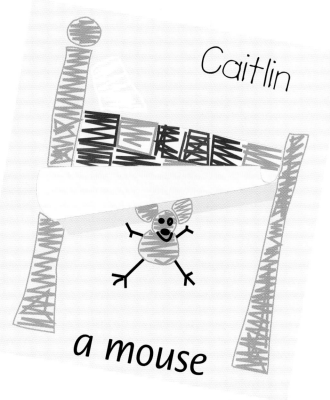

Help little ones identify patterns when they create a colorful sticky-note quilt. Give each child a sticky note and crayons. Invite him to color his note any color he likes. Then encourage all your students to stick their notes to a chalkboard or wall space, placing the notes side by side in a quilt design. When everyone has added his note, ask the children if they see any patterns in the design. Can they move any notes to create or add to a pattern?

Instant Activities With...
The Calendar

ideas contributed by Ada Goren, Angie Kutzer, and Mackie Rhodes

Sunday 1 Apply this timeless letter-recognition activity to your calendar. Simply name a letter; then invite each youngster in turn to find that letter in a word on the calendar. After the child locates the named letter, ask her to name a word that begins with the letter's sound. This idea never ages!

Monday 2 Reinforce recognition of the days of the week with this song. To begin, label each of seven sheets of paper with a different day; then give each of seven students one of the labeled sheets. Direct those students to sequence themselves in a row facing the class. Sing this song, using a different child's name each time the song is repeated. Invite the named child to point to the day of his choice on the calendar, then to find and replace the child holding the corresponding sheet.

(sung to the tune of "The Farmer In The Dell")

[Child's Name] picks a day.
[Child's Name] picks a day.
Heigh-Ho, the Derry-O!
[Child's Name] picks a day.

Tuesday 3 Use this idea to give youngsters practice in number sequencing. Remove a few numerals from the calendar, being sure to leave the numeral *1* in place. Invite a different volunteer to return a numeral to its correct position until all the numerals have been replaced. Then repeat the process using different numerals. As a variation, switch the position of two numerals; then invite a volunteer to find and position the misplaced numerals in the correct order.

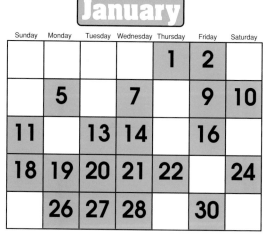

January

Sunday	Monday	Tuesday	Wednesday	Thursday	Friday	Saturday
				1	2	
	5		7		9	10
11		13	14		16	
18	19	20	21	22		24
	26	27	28		30	

Wednesday 4 Youngsters will quickly conquer calendar skills when you use this activity during your extra moments in class. Ask a calendar-related question—such as "What is the third Tuesday of this month?" or "On which day is the 14th of the month?" Then invite a volunteer to point to the answer on the calendar and explain or show how he arrived at his answer.

Thursday 5 March into some calendar fun with this idea. Have a line of youngsters march around the room, stopping beside the calendar. Ask the first child to step up to the calendar, point to and tell the day's date, and then tell about one thing he has done or will do on that day. Direct that child to his seat; then continue in the same fashion, until every child in line has had a turn.

Friday 6 Sharpen youngsters' listening skills with this clapping game. Ask a child to whisper a numeral shown on the calendar into your ear. Then have that child clap his hands that number of times. Invite a volunteer to find the calendar numeral representing the number of claps he heard; then ask the first child to name his number. Did his classmate find the correct number? It's as simple as listen and count!

Saturday 7 Here's an action-packed game that will help students remember the days of the week. Assign each child the name of a day; then pair a different action with each day. For example, the action for Monday might be standing on one foot, for Tuesday hopping up and down, and for Wednesday spinning around. To play, point to a day on the calendar, inviting all the youngsters assigned to that day to perform the designated action. Vary the sequence and speed with which you point to the days to keep the game moving. What a fun way to move through the week!

Today is
Monday
19

Sunday 8 This adaptation of a traditional game will help reinforce youngsters' understanding of the concepts *yesterday* and *tomorrow*. Explain to students that they will play a game similar to Duck, Duck, Goose. To play, position students for the game; then have It circle the seated children, substituting *today* for *duck* and either *yesterday* or *tomorrow* for the catchword *goose*. The child tapped on the catchword becomes the Chaser. After the chase, the child left standing points to the day on the calendar that represents the catchword. Continue the game as interest and time dictate.

December
1st

November
1st

October
1st

July

August
1st

September
1st

153

Instant Activities With...
Duplo® Blocks

ideas contributed by Linda Gordetsky

How do your class blocks measure up? Youngsters will discover the answer to this question when they participate in this activity. To begin, sort your Duplo® block collection into sets by size. Have each child use the same set of blocks to measure a named item. After each child reports his findings, have him use a different block set to measure the same item. Did it take more or fewer blocks from the second set? Guide students to understand that the size of the blocks influences the number needed for measuring different items.

Concentrate youngsters' efforts on matching and visual-memory skills with this game. Randomly place five or more different pairs of matching Duplo® blocks on the floor; then cover each block with a sheet of paper. Invite a small group of students to play a traditional game of Concentration by uncovering two blocks at a time in search of matches.

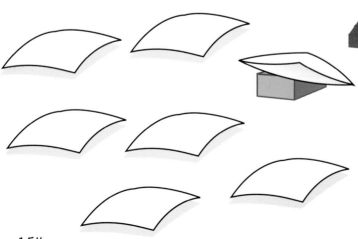

There's no comparison—this block activity is stacked with learning opportunities! To begin, divide your class into student pairs. Give each child in a pair a set of ten connected Duplo® blocks to hold behind his back. On a signal, have each child separate his blocks into two stacks, then place the blocks from his left (or right) hand in front of him. Challenge the pair to compare the number of blocks in each stack to decide which contains the most. For added difficulty, ask the students to determine which partner has the stack with the most blocks remaining behind his back.

Use Duplo® blocks and a container to shake up some fun with making approximations. Simply have a child place an unknown number of blocks into a container. Ask her to shake the container so that her classmates can hear the blocks. Then challenge the class to guess the number of blocks in the container. After the guesses have been made, have the child pour out and count the blocks. Then repeat the activity, inviting the student with the correct or closest guess to take a turn filling the container.

Wheel youngsters into some simple physics discoveries with this block idea. Invite small groups of youngsters to design and build Duplo® block vehicles on Duplo® block wagon bases. Then have the groups explore how smoothly or how quickly their vehicles move along different surfaces—such as tile, carpet, and pavement. If desired, provide block ramps for additional experimentation. Then have students discuss their discoveries. Afterward challenge groups to rebuild their vehicles and repeat the experiment to see if they obtain the same results. It's just simple physics and fantastic fun!

Give youngsters hands-on practice with these Duplo® block bar graphs. To begin, decide on the different categories to be graphed—such as students wearing shoes with laces, shoes with Velcro® straps, shoes with buckles, or just slip-on shoes. Then have a different volunteer create a block tower—or bar—to represent the number in each category. Encourage youngsters to compare the heights of the bars, then share their findings with the class.

Here's a block construction idea that will promote ingenuity and imagination. To begin, sort your Duplo® block collection by colors. Divide your class into small groups; then have each group build a structure using a set of blocks. Invite each group in turn to describe its creation—naming the structure, explaining how it might be used, and telling who might use it and where it might be found. Ready for some creativity? Start building!

Provide each child in a student pair with an identical set of Duplo® blocks. Ask one partner to create a structure with her block set; then challenge her partner to reproduce the structure. Have the pair compare their structures to check for, and correct, any differences. Then invite the partners to switch roles and repeat the activity. There's a duplicate Duplo® delight in every turn!

Instant Activities With...
COOKIE CUTTERS

ideas contributed by Jan Brennan and Mackie Rhodes

Encourage youngsters to connect cookie cutters to your class into small groups; then give a cookie cutter to each child. Have each group make up a story, incorporating the name of each cutter assigned to its members. Then ask each group to sequence and tape together its cookie cutters (in train fashion) to correspond to its story. Invite the groups to use the sequenced cutters to retell their stories to the class.

Heads up for some cookie-cutter relay fun! To play, divide your class into two teams; then establish a starting and a turn-around point for each team. Explain that each team member will, in turn, balance a cookie cutter on her head as she walks to the turn-around point and then back to the start line. After returning to her team, she will pass the cookie cutter to the next player to do the same. If a player drops her cookie cutter, have her replace it on her head before proceeding with the game. Invite the winning team to perform a champion's cookie-cutter cha-cha!

Use this cookie-cutter idea to promote memory skills. Show students a set of five to ten different cookie cutters (depending on your students' abilities); then cover the set with a large sheet of paper and remove one of the cutters. Lift the paper so that youngsters can see the remaining cookie cutters. Ask a volunteer to name the removed cutter. If desired, increase the difficulty level by removing more than one cookie cutter at a time.

The "sillies" will break out in epidemic proportions when youngsters play this giddy little word game. Give each child a different cookie cutter. Recite a well-known rhyme—such as "One, Two, Buckle My Shoe" or "Hey, Diddle Diddle"—omitting the last word of each line in the rhyme. Invite a different child to replace each omitted word with the name of his cookie cutter. The results? A spread of silly sayings that only contagious laughter can cure!

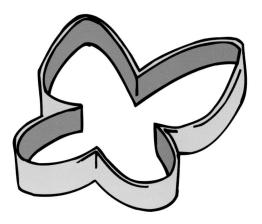

Challenge youngsters' listening skills with a cookie-cutter version of Simon Says. To begin, give each child a cookie cutter; then explain that you will name an action for the child to perform with her cookie cutter, such as "put your cookie cutter on your head" or "hop around your cookie cutter." If you begin the command with "Simon says," the child should perform the action. Otherwise the child should remain still and wait for the next Simon Says command. "Simon says…listen!"

Youngsters will have the opportunity to refine their reasoning abilities with this game of charades. To play, have a student select a cookie cutter out of her classmates' view; then ask her to act out the name of the cutter until a classmate guesses the identity of it. If students have difficulty guessing the name of the cookie cutter, allow the actress to give clues—such as the beginning letter sound of the word or a rhyming word—until a correct guess is made.

Introduce some rhythm into your cookie-cutter activities with this idea. Give each child two cookie cutters, reserving a pair of cutters for yourself. Tap a simple rhythm with your cutters, in wood-block style; then invite students to repeat the rhythm using their cookie cutters in the same fashion. After several rounds, invite student volunteers to take turns creating rhythmic patterns for the class to imitate. Get that cookie-cutter beat when a pair of cutters meet!

If you have a large assortment of cookie cutters, invite youngsters to use them to practice sorting skills. Invite a small group of students to sort the class collection of cookie cutters by common characteristics, such as by function (things that you ride in or eat) or by color. After the group has completed its sorting, ask volunteers to explain why each cutter belongs to the category under which it was grouped.

Instant Activities With...
Shoes

ideas contributed by Linda Gordetsky and Suzanne Moore

Help your youngsters explore positional relationships. Ask each child to remove one shoe. Then give a series of verbal directions for students to follow, such as those below.

- Put your shoe on the table.
- Put your shoe under the table.
- Hold your shoe above your head.
- Put your shoe beside the table leg.
- Put your hand in your shoe.
- Put your hand on the bottom of your shoe.

Compare the various patterns found on the bottoms of your students' shoes. First have each child remove one of her shoes. Demonstrate how to make a rubbing of a shoe bottom by placing a sheet of white or manila paper over the bottom, then rubbing the side of an unwrapped crayon over the paper until the design appears. Invite each child to make a rubbing of her own shoe; then post all the rubbings on a bulletin board for students to examine. Are any of the patterns alike?

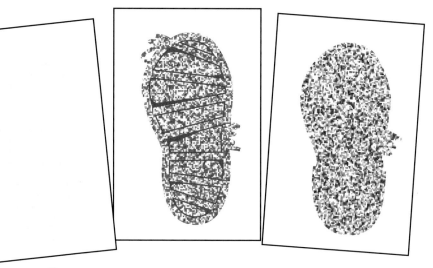

Have your little ones take off their shoes and put them on—their hands! Then engage in some hand dancing, sure to inspire creativity and giggles galore! Invite each child to wear her shoes on her hands and stand beside a table. Play some lively music and encourage each child to dance her hands across the tabletop.

Ask each youngster to remove one shoe. Invite each student to compare her shoe size with a classmate's by holding her shoe sole-to-sole with the other person's shoe. Ask each child to find others with the same shoe size as hers. Extend this activity by having students order their shoes from smallest to largest.

clap, clap

This shoe is black. It has straps and words on it.

red blue yellow
yellow   red
blue

Each of your little ones will be amazed when he discovers a magic egg floating in the air in front of him! To achieve this optical illusion, have each child remove both his shoes and hold them toe-to-toe about one foot in front of his face. Instruct him not to stare directly at his shoe tips, but just beyond them. Can he see the floating egg that appears to be suspended between the shoe tips? The egg will be the same color as his shoes; can he explain why?

Use shoes to explore sound patterns. Ask each child to take off both her shoes and put them on her hands. Let little ones explore the sounds made by clapping the shoes together or slapping them on a tabletop—both one and two at a time. Then use your own shoes to clap and slap a pattern for youngsters to copy, using their newfound shoe sounds.

Encourage youngsters to look and listen carefully as they play this game. Begin by asking each child to remove one of his shoes. Have him examine his shoe carefully, noting its color, how it fastens, any adornments on it, and if there are any words printed on it. Then have all the children deposit their shoes in a large container. Teach the children the chant below; then have a volunteer remove one shoe from the container. Without letting his classmates see the shoe, have the volunteer describe it in detail. The owner of the shoe should claim it as hers. Continue until all the children have their shoes back.

I've got shoes. You've got shoes.
All of these children have shoes.
Some have buckles and some have bows,
But all of them have heels and toes.

159

Instant Activities With...
SEASHELLS

ideas contributed by Angie Kutzer and Suzanne Moore

Give each student a seashell. Have him touch his shell and observe its shape, texture, color, and size. Make a list of the child's descriptions along with his classmates' observations.

It's time for seashell seriating! Divide your students into small groups. Give each group a supply of seashells. Challenge the students to work together to order the shells from the smallest to the largest.

Your youngsters will be wondering who's got the shell in this musical guessing game. Have students stand in a circle. Designate one child to be the Guesser and one child to be the Hider. Give the Hider a small shell and ask the Guesser to stand in the center of the circle. Instruct the remaining students to cup their hands in front of them. Play some beach tunes and direct the Hider to pretend to drop the shell in each child's hands, actually give the shell to a child of his choice, and continue pretending until the music stops. When the music stops, have the children chant, "Shell, shell, who's got the seashell?" Invite the Guesser to try her luck at guessing who has the shell. Then have the Guesser become the Hider and the child with the shell become the next Guesser.

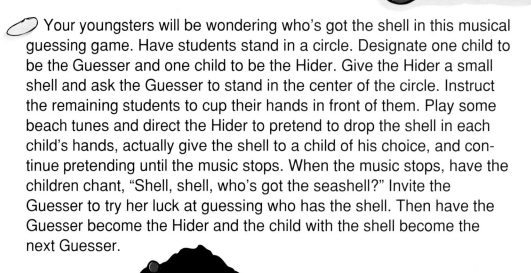

Hide a small shell under one of three large shells. Mix up the shells; then have a student guess which large shell is hiding the smaller shell. If possible, distribute three large shells and one small shell to each small group of three or four children. Encourage the students in each group to take turns mixing and guessing.

Give each student a seashell. Have him use markers or crayons to decorate his shell. Display this unique, colorful collection on a tabletop. Pick one shell to describe. Give clues such as "I see a shell that's green and orange. It has dots. It is above the red shell." Invite a student volunteer to point out the shell that you described. Continue until each child has had a turn to find a shell.

Encourage each child to estimate how many seashells are in your collection. Record the responses; then count the shells aloud with your children to see whose estimate is closest.

Use small seashells to provide a textural touch to the alphabet. Label each of several sheets of heavy paper with a different letter. Then encourage volunteers to trace the outlines with glue and attach shells so that they are touching one another. After the glue dries, pick a letter card. Have a volunteer close her eyes, feel the letter, and guess its name.

Do you have five shells? That's all you need to perform the following counting rhyme. Arrange the shells in a row; then teach your little ones this catchy verse.

Five sandy seashells down by the shore.
One washed away, so then there were four.
Four sandy seashells close to the sea.
One washed away, so then there were three.
Three sandy seashells near the waters blue.
One washed away, so then there were two.
Two sandy seashells shining in the sun.
Another washed away, so that left one.
One sandy seashell as pretty as can be.
I put it in my bucket just for me!

Instant Activities With...
Pattern Blocks

ideas contributed by Vicki Pacchetti

Invite youngsters to play this variation of Go Fish using pattern blocks instead of playing cards. Divide your students into small groups; then divide your supply of pattern blocks equally between the groups. Have each player, without looking, draw seven blocks from the group's container. (Encourage the players to hold their blocks in their laps so that the other players can't see them.) Instruct each player to look at his blocks to see if there are any matching pairs. If so, have him lay the matching pairs on the table.

To begin play, the first player asks another player of his choice for a block to match one of his remaining blocks. If the other player has the designated block, she gives it to the first player. He then lays his matching pair down and repeats this procedure for another block. When a player does not have the block asked for, the first player must draw a block, without looking, from the container and his turn is over. Play continues until one player discards all of his pattern blocks. At that point, all players count the number of pairs they formed. The player with the most matches wins the game.

Demonstrate the concepts of *same* and *different* in this creative activity. Have each student use only two of each of the pattern-block shapes to create a unique design. After everyone finishes, invite youngsters to view their classmates' work. Children will marvel at how many *different* creations can be made with the *same* blocks.

Encourage students to cut corners in completing this pattern-block contest. Divide your group into pairs. Have each child choose three pattern blocks. Instruct him to make a design with the blocks, then count the corners in his design. Have the partners compare their corner counts to determine who has fewer, which makes him the winner. Challenge the pair to rearrange their designs and count the corners again.

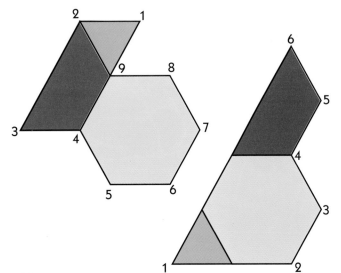

Help your little ones arrange pattern blocks into pattern paths. Begin the activity by demonstrating several patterns with the blocks and having volunteers extend the patterns. Explain that a path is similar to a sidewalk in that there are no spaces in between the sections. Then encourage each youngster to try to make his own pattern path by creating a pattern and repeating it several times. For a more difficult challenge, have youngsters try to create a pattern path that eventually winds around to meet its own beginning.

Give youngsters an opportunity to make and test their predictions using this pattern-block activity. Hold up a pattern-block shape and ask students how many green triangles they think it will take to cover the surface of the shape. After several predictions are made, have a volunteer complete the task and report his findings. Repeat this procedure with other shapes; then challenge the group to sequence the shapes according to the number of triangles it takes to cover them.

Give each pair of students a supply of pattern blocks. Have each pair work together to build a hexagon-shaped tower. To begin, place one of the yellow hexagon blocks on the table between the partners to be the base of the tower. Then instruct each partner to build another hexagon shape on top of the base using a combination of the other blocks. Encourage the two students to take turns, with each child building alternating levels until no more hexagons can be made.

Invite your little ones to become fence builders. Have each child place pattern blocks on their edges to build a fence. (Wooden pattern blocks can be stacked two or three blocks high.) Challenge her to keep her fence's design consistent throughout its entire length.

163

Instant Activities With...

BOOKS

ideas contributed by Barbara Backer and Angie Kutzer

Select a book that you have not read to your class. Show the pictures one by one and encourage students to create a story line. Then read the actual story to the children. Discuss the similarities and differences between the students' and the author's ideas.

After reading a book to your youngsters, give each child a piece of paper. Challenge the child to draw a picture that changes the ending to the story or tells what happens next. Invite each child to share her story extension with the group.

Use books to search for alphabet treasures. Have each child choose a book from the class library, then sit in a circle. Ask a volunteer to write a letter of her choice on the chalkboard. Have the rest of the group identify the letter, then search for it in their books. Encourage each child to show his find to the children seated next to him. Choose another volunteer and continue the search.

Read aloud two versions of a classic tale. Encourage children to describe the similarities and differences between the two stories. Divide a sheet of paper in half. Write each title on a different half of the paper; then tally votes to find out which version was the class favorite.

Use books to practice rhyming words. Show students a page from any picture book. Have each child name a different object on the page, then give a word that rhymes with the object. Accept any rhyming word, even nonsense ones. Pounce, "hounce," "dounce," it's the rhyme that counts!

Here's a chance for children to size up the books in the classroom library. Ask a volunteer to find a small book and display it in front of the group. Ask another volunteer to find a book that's a little larger than the first book and place it next to the first. Continue in this manner until no larger books can be found. Then mix up the displayed collection, have a volunteer pick out the largest book, and direct her to put it back on the shelf. Continue having the children locate smaller and smaller books until all of the books are put away.

Use those few extra minutes to reinforce students' knowledge of the concepts of print. Give each child a book. Direct him to listen closely and follow your directions. Then call out directions such as "Point to the front cover of the book. Point to a word in the book. Where is the title page? Show me where you begin reading a page."

Provide a variety of books for children to sort into their own categories or into the categories shown here.

- pictures on the cover/no pictus on the cover
- stories with animals/stories without animals
- large books/small books
- real stories/make-believe stories
- colored pictures/black-and-white pictures
- lots of words in text/a few words in text

Instant Activities With...

ideas contributed by Ada Goren, Angie Kutzer, and Mackie Rhodes

Seat students in a circle. Bring to the circle two containers, one of which is partially filled with sand. Give one volunteer the container with sand. Then give the empty container to the child on the volunteer's left. Have the first volunteer say the first word in a sequence—such as "one," "a," "Monday," or "January." After saying the word, direct him to pour the sand into the empty container and give his container to the child on the other side of the second volunteer. Direct the second volunteer to say the second word of the established sequence, then repeat the sand-pouring routine. Continue in this manner until the sequence ends or the sand travels all the way around the circle.

Gather a group of little ones around your sand table. Show students a bucket (or other container) and shovel. Invite each child to estimate how many scoops of sand it will take to fill the bucket. Then have each child take a turn putting a scoop of sand in the bucket while the remaining students count aloud.

Oh, those lazy days of summer! Have children describe real or imagined vacations to the beach. Then give each child a sheet of paper and instruct her to draw her favorite beach activity or a decorative beach scene. No beach scene is complete without sand! Invite the child to add glue and sprinkle sand wherever a little texture is needed.

Try this sticky idea for sand! Give each child a length of tape. Have him press his tape into the sand and shake off the excess. Collect students' strips and divide them into three or four sets. Then divide students into the same number of groups. Challenge each group to use a set of strips to create a sandy design. Invite each group to share its design with the rest of the class.

Ahoy, mate! Methinks me spies a buried treasure! Label each of several small pieces of paper with a different letter, numeral, or shape. Bury these pieces in the sand. Encourage little ones to dig in and find one of the pieces. When a piece is found, have the child identify it, then bury it again for another petite pirate to find.

Here's the scoop on a great relay. Set the sand table in the middle of an open area. Put a chair the same distance away from both ends of the table. Divide your group into two teams. To play the game, the first member from each team takes a scoopful of sand, walks around his team's designated chair, goes back to the table, dumps the sand, and takes the scoop to the next team member. Play continues until every member of the faster team has had a turn. Then the winning team sits while the losing team sweeps!

Encourage critical thinking and problem solving by asking small groups of students to redistribute the sand that's in the box or table in the following ways:

Divide the sand so that
- one side of the box has more/less than the other side.
- both sides have the same amount of sand.
- all four corners of the container have the same amount, but the middle has none.
- the corners of the container have none and the middle has all of the sand.

All of this sand is bound to stir up some hunger. Encourage your little ones to use their imaginations to create delectable sandy sundaes. Give each child a container. Instruct the child to fill the container with a scoop of ice cream (sand), then take it outside to the garnish bar. Once outside, direct the child to look around for possible toppings such as grass sprinkles, rocky chocolate chips, leaf cream, and cookie sticks. Yum! Yum!

Instant Activities With...
BEANBAGS

ideas contributed by Diane Gilliam, Linda Gordetsky, and Mackie Rhodes

Keep youngsters alert with this beanbag circle game. Invite a volunteer to demonstrate an action using a beanbag—such as placing the bag on her head and clapping her hands twice—then to pass the beanbag to the next child. Have that child imitate the first child's action. Continue the game until every child has had a turn; then invite a different volunteer to begin the game again using a different action.

Bag some measuring skills with this idea. Divide your class into small groups of students; then give a sheet of paper and a marker to an appointed recorder in each group. Have each group use beanbags to measure items in the classroom—such as the length of a tabletop or the width of a cubby space—and report its findings to the recorder. Then invite each group to share its results with the class.

Here's an idea you'll not want to pass up! Seat youngsters in a circle; then invite a volunteer to hold a beanbag while he briefly tells the class about a personal experience—such as his first solo bike ride or an excursion to the circus. After that child relates his story, have him toss the beanbag to a classmate. Encourage the classmate to follow suit with an experience of his own. If he chooses not to share a story, have him say, "Pass," then toss the beanbag to another child. Continue in this fashion, giving every child an opportunity to tell a story.

Create a beanbag graph to provide youngsters with practice in counting and making comparisons. To begin, label (or illustrate) a separate sheet of paper with each different category to be graphed, such as clothing colors or favorite sports; then create a floor graph by positioning the sheets side by side. Invite each child to place a beanbag on the graph according to his response. Afterward compare and discuss the results with students.

Youngsters will delight in passing classified information when they engage in this activity. Seat students in a circle; then name a category, such as animals, colors, or transportation. Give a child a beanbag, directing him to name an item belonging in the category. Then have him pass the beanbag to the next student. Continue the game, encouraging each child to name a different item from the category until a child is unable to name a different item. Then repeat the game, using a different category.

Try this beanbag toss game to fill in some extra time. Gather several sheets of construction paper corresponding to each beanbag color. Arrange the papers in a large circle on the floor; then tape a sheet of paper in the middle of the circle. Invite each child, in turn, to stand on the paper inside the circle and toss each of three beanbags onto a matching sheet of paper. Each time his beanbag lands on a target, ask the child to name an item of the same color. What colorful thinking!

Have youngsters play this snaky game to practice their listening skills. Give each child a beanbag; then ask the class to pattern their beanbags by color to create a snake. After the snake is complete, explain that you will name a child and an action—such as, "Cameron, jump over the snake." Invite the child to perform the action, then return to the group. Continue the game, giving every child an opportunity to play. So, lis-s-sten clos-s-sely—you might be next!

Have youngsters sort your collection of beanbags by color; then divide the class into as many groups as the number of beanbag colors. Assign a different-color beanbag for each student group to divide into sets of two. Ask each group to skip-count its beanbags, then report its findings to the class. Then have each group exchange beanbags with another group and repeat the activity.

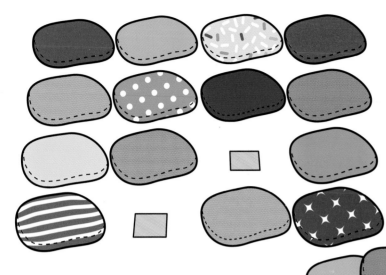

 Engage youngsters in a beanbag memory game to reinforce visual memory and matching skills. To set up the game, prepare several different pairs of construction-paper shapes. Or gather several pairs of small objects from the classroom. Place each item under a separate beanbag so that it cannot be seen; then have youngsters play a traditional game of Concentration, looking under the beanbags for the matching items. After all the matches have been found, set up the playing area for another round of play.

Stack up some storytelling skills with this beanbag idea. To begin, give each child a beanbag, keeping one for yourself. Place your beanbag on the floor and say a story-starting sentence such as, "I took my dog for a walk in the park." Invite a volunteer to stack his beanbag on top of yours, then add a sentence to the story. Have each child in turn do the same, until all the beanbags are stacked or until the stack falls over. Then begin another story in the same fashion.

Promote letter and sound associations with this circle game. Say a word; then toss a beanbag to a student. Ask the child to identify the beginning letter of that word. (Give her clues, as necessary, to help her identify the correct letter.) After she answers correctly, have her toss the beanbag back to you. Then repeat the process so that each child has a turn to name a letter.

 Here's a quick activity to help students solve simple word problems. Provide a supply of beanbags; then present simple word problems involving addition or subtraction for youngsters to solve. Encourage students to use the beanbags to set up each problem, and to manipulate the beanbags to arrive at a solution. As each problem is solved, ask the students to share their results with the class.

I had four bones. I ate three of them. How many bones do I have left?

Toss around some sequencing and turn-taking skills with this partner game. Give each student pair a beanbag; then instruct the partners to toss the bag back and forth to each other while reciting the alphabet (or numbers in a number sequence). Encourage the partners to name one letter (or number) per toss. Have the pair continue until an incorrect response is given or the sequence is completed. Then invite them to repeat the game, trying to correctly complete the sequence at a faster rate.

Try this little twist on using beanbags to give youngsters some big experiences in making size comparisons. Give each child a beanbag; then ask him to find an object that is smaller than the beanbag. Invite each child in turn to share his finding with the class. Then repeat the activity, this time challenging students to find an object larger than—or the same size as—the beanbag.

For a fast, fun way to reinforce counting skills, this relay game can't be beat. Divide your class into two teams; then divide your beanbag supply evenly between the teams. Instruct the leader of each team to arrange a beanbag path from a designated starting point to a finish line. Explain that each team member will count the beanbags as he follows his team's path to the finish line. The last player on each team will gather his team's bags and deliver them to the finish line, where the entire team will chorally count them. Did every team member get the same results? Repeat the game as often as interest and time dictate. On your mark…get set…count!

Hot, warm, or cold—youngsters will control the temperature of this beanbag search game. To play, ask a volunteer to hide a beanbag; then appoint another child to be the beanbag hunter. Encourage the hider to use the terms *hot, warm,* and *cold* to clue the hunter on her proximity to the hidden beanbag (with *hot* indicating *close* to the bag and *cold* meaning *farther away). After the hunter finds the bag, invite her to hide the beanbag; then repeat the game, selecting a different child to be the hunter. Getting cold? Just move around to find a hot spot!

Instant Activities With...
BUBBLES AND BLOWERS

ideas contributed by Ada Goren, Angie Kutzer, and Mackie Rhodes

Provide each student with a bubble blower and some bubble solution. Call out a number between one and five. Challenge each youngster to blow a set of bubbles to match the designated number.

After some free-exploration time with blowing bubbles, give each child a sheet of paper. Direct her to draw a picture of where she imagines her bubble traveling. If time permits, write each child's dictated sentence on her picture.

What's better than bumper cars and bumper boats? Bumping bubbles, of course! Divide your students into pairs. Have each pair sit across from one another. Have the partners blow bubbles simultaneously and try to make them bump into each other. Do the bubbles bounce back, or do they break?

Challenge each child to blow a bubble, then catch it on his blower. As a variation, have pairs of students work together. Instruct one partner to blow a bubble, then hand the blower to the other partner. Encourage the other partner to use the blower to catch the bubble. Direct the pairs to count the number of successful catches.

Round up your little bubble busters for this movement activity. Divide your students into small groups. Have one group stand in an open area. Blow a whole breath of bubbles and challenge the group to pop all of them. Encourage the other groups to watch closely to see if any bubbles get away. Then switch groups for another round of bubbles.

Use your blower to tap rhythm patterns against your bottle of bubble solution. Encourage students to repeat the rhythms with their blowers and bottles. At the end of each successful imitation, show a pattern of "dip, pucker, blow" so that children can celebrate with a breath of bubbles.

Ask two volunteers to stand side by side and blow a breath of bubbles at the same time. Have the remaining students compare to see who blew more or fewer bubbles.

Following directions using bubbles is fun! Have each child listen carefully as you call out directions such as those shown here.

Blow bubbles up/down.
Blow bubbles to the left/right.
Blow bubbles while you stand on one foot/tiptoes.
Blow bubbles with your eyes closed.
Blow bubbles with a strong breath/soft breath.
Blow one big bubble.
Blow lots of little bubbles.

Tape two parallel lines on the floor a short distance from each other. Explain to students that the goal of this activity is to get a bubble from one line to the other before it pops. Have each child stand at one of the lines and blow a bubble towards the other line. Encourage him to follow his bubble with more gentle blowing if necessary.

Instant Activities With...
PAPER CUPS

ideas contributed by Ada Goren and Carrie Lacher

Play a preschool version of the old shell game. Invert three or four paper cups on a tabletop. Show your students a small object, such as a paper clip. Ask students to watch very closely. Slide the object under one of the cups; then move the cups around, changing their positions. Invite a volunteer to guess which cup is hiding the object. If he guesses correctly, let him hide the object and move the cups for the next round of play.

Bring out a supply of paper cups for youngsters to use as building blocks. Little ones will delight in building tall towers and pyramids and you won't have to worry when the lightweight cups fall over!

Engage youngsters in an exploration of feelings. Begin by singing a round of "If You're Happy And You Know It"; then discuss the many feelings we can have and how expressions show our feelings. Provide each child with a paper cup, a sheet of paper, and crayons. Demonstrate how to trace around the rim of a cup to make a circle. Then ask each student to draw a face inside the circle that represents her current feelings. When everyone has finished drawing, seat youngsters in a circle in your group area. Teach children the chant below; then give each child a chance to show her drawing and tell about her feelings.

Round and round and round, we say;
Tell us how you feel today.

Ask each youngster to pick a partner; then provide each pair with a paper cup and a pair of scissors. Demonstrate for each pair how to cut down the side of the cup, then cut off the cup bottom to create a disk. Have each child write his first name on one side of his pair's disk. Then have each pair take turns flipping its disk by pressing down on one edge. The child whose name lands on top gets the next turn to flip the disk. If desired, have older children use tally marks to keep track of how many times their names are flipped to the top.

Don't let the leftover paper cup go to waste! Show youngsters how to cut the remaining semicircle in half lengthwise, creating two cuff bracelets, one for each child in the pair to wear.

Tap into patterning practice when you use paper cups as drums. Give each child a paper cup and—if desired—a pencil. Have each youngster invert her cup on the tabletop. Then tap out a pattern on your own cup (using your fingertip or a pencil) and ask your students to copy it by tapping on their paper-cup drums. Sounds like fun!

Transform paper cups into spyglasses for this beginning-sounds activity. Assist each child in cutting or punching out the bottom of a paper cup. Then ask him to name a letter he knows. Print the letter on the side of his cup. Then ask him to look through his newly made spyglass and search for items in your classroom that begin with the sound of his chosen letter. If desired, print the names of the objects he spies on the side of his cup. To extend the activity, have students switch spyglasses and hunt for objects with different sounds.

These crew-cut puppets are the cutest! For each child, provide a paper cup, scissors, and crayons. Help each youngster cut or punch out the bottom of his cup. Then have him draw a face on his cup, positioning the cup so that the missing cup bottom is the top of the puppet. Then invite each child to slip his hand inside his cup and use his fingers to simulate the puppet's hair. For a variation, have youngsters make bug or bunny puppets, using two fingers to create antennae or ears.

Instant Activities With...
Markers

ideas contributed by Ada Goren, Angie Kutzer, and Mackie Rhodes

Have your little ones put on their thinking caps for this game of color clues! Invite one child to select a marker from your collection without the other children seeing his choice. Have him hide the marker behind his back and give clues about the color until someone guesses correctly.

Use markers to give your students practice with following directions. For younger children, distribute two different-color markers to each child. Give directions such as "If you have a red marker, tap it on your knee," or "If you have a blue marker, touch it to your nose." For older children, give each child a sheet of paper and a selection of markers. Give directions such as "Draw a red *X* in the center of your paper," or "Draw a purple flower in one corner."

Your little artists can produce some beautiful underwater scenes using crayons and watercolor markers. Give each child a sheet of paper and crayons. Have her draw an underwater scene—perhaps goldfish in a bowl or her favorite ocean critter. Then provide blue and green watercolor markers and encourage each child to color over her drawing. This activity is sure to make a big splash!

If you have some dried-up markers lying around, use the lids to create finger puppets. Invite each child to draw a character and cut it out. Then tape the cut-out drawing to a marker lid and have the child slip it onto her finger. Encourage small groups of little ones to make up stories they can perform with their finger puppets.

If you have markers with correspondingly colored lids, try this simple activity. Remove the lids from a number of markers equal to one-half of your class. Distribute either a marker or a lid to each child. Then encourage each child to find her partner—the child with the corresponding marker or lid. If time permits, have the partners sit together and draw a cooperative picture using a selection of markers.

Snap together two or three markers to create a long magic wand. Invite a child to tap a classmate with the wand and tell something positive about him. Then use another marker to draw a smiley face on the tapped child's hand to remind him of the "happy spell" he is under!

Markers and lids make instant ink stamps! Give each child a sheet of paper and a lidded marker. Demonstrate how to color the top of the lid with a marker, and then turn the lid over and stamp a circle on the paper. Then allow each child to make a design of circles all over her paper. Or—for a more directed activity—ask each child to write a numeral on her paper, then stamp a corresponding number of circles next to it. Continue as time permits.

Give each child a sheet of paper and a marker. Explain that the children are going to draw pictures and that you have a way for them to share the markers. Tell them that when you say "pop," each child may pop the top off her marker and begin drawing. When you say "stop," she replaces the lid on her marker. And when you say "swap," she passes her marker to the child beside her. Then she may begin again with a new marker. Pop, stop, swap—drawing this way is fun!

Instant Activities With...

ideas contributed by Vicki Pacchetti

◇ Travel back to medieval times with the roll of a die. Seat your class in a circle. Have one child at a time roll a die to test his luck. If he rolls a one, he goes to the dungeon (center of the circle)—any other number keeps him safe. The captives are released from the dungeon whenever a classmate rolls a six. Then everyone inside is free to return to the circle to resume rolling.

◇ Start a story circle by rolling a die (or dice) and making up a story starter that uses the number rolled. For example, if you rolled a three you might say, "Three days ago...." Pass the die to the next child and have her repeat the procedure, extending the story with another number-filled sentence. Continue until everyone has had a turn.

◇ Use dice to work on sequencing skills. Give each child a die; then divide the class into groups of four. Have the members of each group roll their dice. Encourage the group to work together to sequence the dice from the smallest to the largest number.

◇ Divide your class into small groups. Give a die to each group. Have each member of the group gaze into the "crystal cube" and predict what number will be rolled. After everyone makes a prediction, invite one child to roll the die. Were any predictions correct? Continue until each member has had a turn to roll the die.

⬧ Pair up students and let the dice duels begin! Give each pair of partners a piece of paper, a pencil, and four dice. Instruct each partner to roll two of the dice. Have them count and compare their rolls to find out who rolled the largest sum, and thus, won the round. Encourage more advanced students to keep a tally of the winner of each round. Touché!

⬧ Use this dice activity to practice graphing and comparing data. Make graph headings by labeling each of six pieces of construction paper with a different number from one to six. Arrange the headings in a row on the floor. Have each child roll a die, then stand above the corresponding number heading. When everyone is incorporated in the graph, count and discuss the results.

⬧ Shake up your youngsters' exercise routine by letting the dice sergeants decide the number of repetitions to do. Have a volunteer name an exercise. Then direct another volunteer to roll the dice to find out how many times the class will do the exercise. "Now drop and give us 12!"

⬧ Get youngsters rolling with this catchy rhyme. Teach the verse; then divide students into small groups. Give each group a pair of dice and encourage them to count how many rolls it takes to roll two of a kind.

Wiggle, jiggle, shake the dice.
Roll them once; roll them twice.
Try again; don't get behind.
Can you roll two of a kind?

Instant Activities With...
Yarn

ideas contributed by Ada Goren, Angie Kutzer, Linda Ludlow, and Mackie Rhodes

Create a yarn path on your classroom floor. Tape it in place. Then invite your little ones to perform specified actions along the path—such as hopping, tiptoeing, crawling, or marching.

All you need is one short length of yarn to play this game. Choose one child to be the Birdie and ask her to turn her back to the group. Give a short length of yarn—a worm—to one child. Then have all the children hold their hands in front of them with fists closed and palms down. Explain that their hands represent the ground and the Birdie is going to hunt for the worm in the ground. Ask the Birdie to turn around and choose a child she thinks has the worm. Have her softly "peck" (with her thumb and forefinger together like a beak) on the chosen child's hand. That child then opens her hand to reveal whether or not the worm is hidden there. As the Birdie searches for the worm, have the other children recite the chant below. If desired, give the Birdie a specified number of tries to find the worm. Have the child who held the worm be the Birdie for the next round.

Birdie, Birdie, searching all around…
Can you find the little worm hiding in the ground?

Give youngsters practice with tying bows. Provide each child with a sheet of paper, crayons, and a manageable length of yarn. Encourage him to draw a picture he'd like to present to a loved one as a gift. When the picture is finished, have him roll it up like a diploma. Then help him wrap the yarn around the center of the roll and tie a bow to hold it in place. (This will be easier if you tape the roll in place first.)

Provide each child with a length of yarn. Ask your students to imagine their pieces of yarn as caterpillars. Have them recite the poem below, moving their yarn caterpillars as you specify different body parts.

Caterpillar crawls on my [knee], silly bug!
His wiggle makes me giggle, so I give my bug a hug!

Encourage youngsters to practice creating sets of one to five with this activity. First give each child a length of yarn. As you call out numbers from one to five, have her wrap the yarn around the specified number of fingers on one of her hands. For further practice, give each child a sheet of paper, a crayon, a pair of scissors, a long length of yarn, and glue. As you count aloud from 1 to 15, have each child draw 15 dots randomly on her paper. Then have her cut lengths of yarn and make loops around her dots, creating sets of one to five. Have her glue the loops in place.

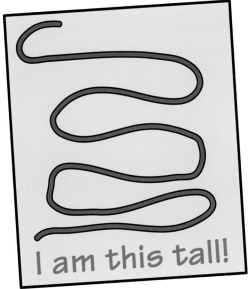

I am this tall!

Have each student pick a partner. Provide each pair with a ball of yarn (or a very long length) and a pair of scissors. Ask the partners to use the yarn to measure one another and cut lengths of yarn equal to each child's height. Then provide paper and glue. Encourage each child to arrange his yarn length on his paper, bending and looping it so that it all fits on the sheet. Then have him glue the yarn down. On each child's paper, write "I am this tall!" Have him take the paper home as a keepsake.

Cut a length of yarn several feet long; then tie the ends together securely. Divide your class into small groups. Ask one group at a time to hold the yarn loop and arrange themselves to form a shape, such as a circle, square, or triangle. Continue, having each group form a different shape.

Instant Activities With...

Newspapers & Magazines

ideas contributed by Angie Kutzer and Carrie Lacher

Provide students with magazines, paper, scissors, and glue for this delicious activity. Discuss with your youngsters the importance of healthful foods. Then have each child search through the magazines and cut out pictures of healthful foods. Encourage her to choose from her cutouts several foods that could make a balanced meal, then glue them to her paper. Assist the child in labeling the different meal components.

Give each child five half sheets of paper and a section of the newspaper. Encourage the child to look for the numerals one through five in print and cut them out. Instruct him to glue each numeral to a different sheet of paper. Then have the child look for sets of objects that match the numerals, cut them out, and glue them to the corresponding pages. Sequence the pages between a folded sheet of construction paper and bind the number booklet together.

Divide your students into small groups and give each group a newspaper section. Challenge each group to work together to find every letter of the alphabet, cut out the letters, and glue them in sequence on a sheet of paper. Anyone see an *X?*

Provide some fine-motor skill practice with the coupon section. Have each child carefully clip a few coupons along the dotted lines. Encourage each child to take home a few coupons for products that his family uses. Mothers will be sure to thank their little helpers for the money-saving discounts.

Add some color to your classroom with magazines. Place one large sheet of each basic color of construction paper on the floor. Have each student look through magazines, cut out objects that match the construction-paper colors, and glue them onto the appropriate sheets of paper. Display the color collages in a row on a classroom wall. Color is all around us!

 Use a magazine picture or newspaper photo as the subject for a whole-group creative-writing session. Glue the picture to a large sheet of construction paper or chart paper. Discuss the picture with your students and brainstorm what might be happening. Then ask each student volunteer to contribute a sentence to a short story about the picture. Read aloud the completed story. If time permits, use the story to practice a few phonemic-awareness strategies or to review the concepts of print.

Scoop up some fun as well as coordination with these news-paper scoops and balls. To make a scoop, fold a double sheet of newspaper in half. Cut a semicircle shape from the paper, making sure that the straight line is along the fold as shown. Roll the half circle into a cone shape so that the folded edge is at the point. Then staple or tape the cone together. Encourage each child to use a scoop to catch and pass small newspaper balls around the room from classmate to classmate. Here, catch!

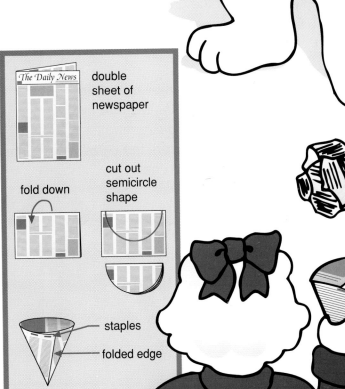

The Daily News

double sheet of newspaper

fold down

cut out semicircle shape

staples

folded edge

We're going on a letter hunt! Label each child's paper with a letter of her choice. Then give her a newspaper or magazine, and direct her to begin her search for the chosen letter. As examples of the letter are found, have the child cut them out and glue them to her paper. After several minutes of searching, call the group back together. Count aloud the number of letters each child found. Discuss why some students may have found more examples than other children.

Instant Activities With...
PLASTIC LINKS

ideas contributed by Ada Goren, Angie Kutzer, and Mackie Rhodes

Put a supply of separated links in a container. Have each child select a link without looking. When everyone has a link, instruct each student to find the others who picked the same-colored link. Ask the color groups to make a chain with their links. Then compare chains to see which group's is the longest, which group's is the shortest, or if two of the groups have the same length chain.

Make a patterned linking chain using seven or eight links. Add an extra link somewhere in the pattern. Then ask students to examine the chain. Have the child who discovers the extra link take it out and reconnect the chain.

Have each child make a crown using plastic links. Instruct her to wear her crown as she performs movements that you call out—such as "Shake one leg," or "Wave your arms in the air." If a child's crown falls off, she sits down until the next round of play. Who's the king or queen of linked movements?

Instruct each child to make a linked chain for each of the numbers one through ten. Mix up the chains; then challenge the child to sequence them in the correct order.

Write a different letter on each of four pieces of paper. Tape the letter cards to the wall in a row; then tape a link under each letter. Give each child a link. Have a volunteer name a word that begins with one of the posted letters; then help him add his link to the link under the appropriate letter. Continue in this manner until everyone has a turn to name and link. Complete the activity by comparing the number of links in each chain.

Invite each youngster to make a long slinky snake with the links. Encourage her to explore different ways to make her snake move by shaking, twisting, swaying, or wiggling her arm and hand.

m   b   s   f

Now that little ones are experienced with linking chains, forget the plastic and try the human link. Have each child hook arms with two other classmates to create a human chain. Then introduce the concept of a *chain reaction.* Have one volunteer bend forward, thus causing the next child to bend and the next child and so on. Continue with other motions, such as leaning back, leaning to the side, and sitting down. Beware, giggles are also a chain reaction!

List each child's estimate of how many links it would take to make a chain that would stretch from one side of the classroom to the other. Then invite students to help you construct a linking chain to check the estimates. Was anyone's guess close?

Instant Activities With...
Dress-Up Clothes & Props

ideas contributed by Ada Goren, Angie Kutzer, Carrie Lacher, and Mackie Rhodes

What do you want to be when you grow up? Give your little ones a chance to answer this question by dressing the part. Begin by discussing the many possibilities for careers—from mommies and daddies to astronauts and presidents. Then invite a few children at a time to select from your assortment of dress-up clothes and props and dress as a worker they'd like to be. Encourage the rest of the children to guess what their costumes represent.

Use your dress-up clothes and props to stimulate a discussion of community helpers. Set out all the clothing and props related to community helpers near your group area. Then gather your students and give them a scenario, such as "Oh, no! We had a bad storm and a tree fell on my house. Which helper do I need?" Invite a volunteer to dress himself as the appropriate helper and tell who he is and what he will do to help. Continue with other scenarios and volunteers.

Seat your students in a circle. Pass around a hat from your community helper costume collection as the children sing the song below. At the end of the verse, have the child holding the hat put it on and tell which helper he is and what he does. Then begin again with another hat.

(sung to the tune of "Three Blind Mice")

Who are you?
Who are you?
What do you do?
What do you do?
Your job's important, we know that's true,
For helping people like me and you.
You wear this hat; that's a very big clue.
Who are you?

Help youngsters develop dramatic-play skills with this pantomime activity. From your collection of dress-up clothes, pull out several items that are put on or fastened in different ways—perhaps a belt, a hat, a necklace, a pullover shirt, a pair of shoes, and a pair of eyeglasses. Then have two children at a time come forward. Instruct one child to look at the selected clothing items and choose one, without picking it up or telling her choice. Then ask her to pantomime putting on that article of clothing—for example, stepping into a pair of pants and zipping them up. Have her partner watch her movements, then select the item he believes she chose and actually put it on. If he guesses correctly, invite him to pantomime putting on another clothing item for a new partner.

Use a toy telephone to give youngsters practice with reciting their addresses. Provide a toy phone (or two if possible) and a phone book. Ask one child to pretend to call and order a pizza. Have another child pretend to answer the call and ask for the delivery address.

Toy telephones are natural tools for practicing telephone manners. Discuss polite ways to answer the phone, ask for someone, and say good-bye, as well as discussing safety issues—such as never telling a caller that parents aren't home. Demonstrate good—and safe—phone manners with the help of a student volunteer and two toy phones. Then let pairs of children use the phones, demonstrating what they've learned.

Here's a fun way to encourage youngsters to discuss a story you've recently shared. Use a toy telephone to place a pretend call to a story character—such as Goldilocks or the Very Hungry Caterpillar. Pretend that the character isn't at home, but has left on his or her answering machine. Encourage the children to leave a message. Pass the toy phone around and have each child tell the character what part of the story she liked or ask a question about the story.

Instant Activities With... STENCILS

ideas contributed by Ada Goren, Angie Kutzer, and Mackie Rhodes

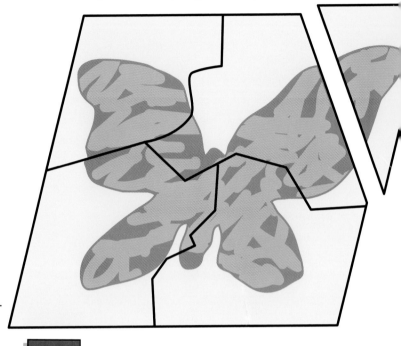

S Stencil puzzles will help youngsters with visual-discrimination and problem-solving skills. Have each child trace and color a stencil picture onto a sheet of construction paper. Then direct the child to cut the picture into an appropriate number of pieces. Encourage students to exchange and solve classmates' puzzles.

S Exercise little ones' fine-motor skills by having each child use letter stencils to write her name on an individual strip of paper. Encourage the child to use markers and crayons to color and embellish her name. Then use the strips as desktags.

S Do you have a variety of stencils? If so, use them as a great sorting activity. Give each child a stencil. Have students work together to group themselves into different categories such as numbers, letters, animals, or vehicles.

S Give each child a numeral stencil. Ask a volunteer to show his stencil and identify the numeral. Then call out an action—such as clapping, winking, or jumping—and direct students to perform the action the designated number of times. Continue until everyone has had a turn to identify his numeral.

S Use animal stencils to spark students' wild imaginations. Demonstrate how to make a fantasy animal by tracing the head, body, and tail of three different animals. (For younger students, trace only two animals—the front half of one and the back half of another.) Then encourage your little ones to create their own wacky wildlife!

S Check to see if students have an eye for spotting identical shapes. Have each child trace and color a different stencil on his sheet of paper. Collect the stencils and the drawings; then redistribute the stencils to different children. Show a colored tracing. Direct the child holding the matching stencil to stand up.

S Discuss habitats and environments with your little ones as you hold up animal stencils one at a time. Then give each child a sheet of paper. Direct him to choose an animal stencil to trace and color. Then instruct him to add an appropriate background for the chosen animal.

S Put on a show of charades by using stencils as cues. Show a volunteer an animal or object stencil. Then have her act out the stencil as classmates guess the stencil's identity. A star is born!

189

Instant Activities With...

Crepe-Paper Streamers

ideas contributed by Angie Kutzer and Joyce Montag

Use crepe-paper streamers for this unique painting technique. Tear an assortment of colorful crepe paper into small two-inch strips. Have each child fingerpaint the entire surface of a piece of white construction paper with water. Then direct her to cover the wet paper with the crepe-paper pieces to create an interesting mosaic design. Or for a more blended look, have the child dip each crepe-paper piece into a dish of water before pressing it to the paper. After the paper dries, lift off the streamer pieces to discover the great crepe painting!

Arrange three 8-foot streamers on the floor. Have a volunteer sit at an end of each streamer and hold it in place. Then have the other children move about the shape by jumping, stepping, or hopping over the streamers. Choose more volunteers to hold the streamers so that everyone has a turn to move between the streamers. For added fun, have the volunteers periodically raise the streamers several inches off the floor. Watch where you step!

Cut a 16-inch crepe-paper streamer for each child. Invite your little ones to use the streamers as they explore the following creative movements; then have children make up some movements of their own.

Twirl like a tornado.   Tiptoe like a fairy.
Zigzag like lightning.   Squiggle like a worm.
Bounce like a spring.   Glide like an eagle.
Slither like a snake.   Flutter like a butterfly.
Snap like a whip.   Hop like a bunny.

Divide your class into small groups of three or four children. Give each child an 18-inch streamer. Call out the name of a letter, number, or shape and challenge the groups to work cooperatively to construct the designated formation with their streamers on the floor.

Only have a few minutes for sharing? Try this idea. Cut half as many four-foot streamers as there are students. Pile all of the streamers into a bundle on the floor, making sure that the ends of each streamer are easily accessible. Direct your students to encircle the streamer pile. On your cue, have each child discover her sharing partner by picking up a streamer's end and carefully walking backwards until the streamer is taut. Have the partners sit together for a few minutes of sharing with one another.

Listening and color-recognition skills will be hard at work in this activity. Choose four rolls of crepe paper that are different colors. Cut 12-inch streamers from the rolls so that each child has two different-colored streamers. Loosely tie one streamer to each wrist of every child. Give directions such as "Red join blue. Green join red. Yellow join blue." Direct each child to join hands with the appropriate classmate according to your directions.

Cut a class supply of streamers in various lengths. Give each child a streamer; then divide the class into small groups. Direct children in each group to order their streamers on the floor from longest to shortest.

Use crepe paper to add a twist to the traditional game of London Bridge. Cut two 36-inch streamers. Have two volunteers hold the streamers' ends so that the strips are taut. With the streamers raised, direct the rest of the class to walk in pairs under the streamers while singing the following song. When the song ends, have the two volunteers lower the streamers to catch a pair of students to take their place.

(sung to the tune of "London Bridge")

With your partner, take a walk,
Take a walk, take a walk.
With your partner, take a walk.
Oops, you're caught!

Catch your little tigers by their tails with this fun game. To prepare, cut a 24-inch paper streamer for all but one child. Choose a volunteer to be the tiger without a tail. Then help each of the other children tuck one end of a streamer under his waistband to represent a tail. Divide your tigers into two groups. Mark a boundary line on each side of your room; then line up one group behind each line.

To play the game, the tailless tiger stands between the lines. On your cue, the two groups of tigers run to their opposite lines while the tailless tiger grabs as many tails as he can. Once everyone is behind the boundary lines, count aloud to see how many tails were pulled. Then help the tailless tiger insert the collected tails under his waistband, and call the new tailless tigers to the middle for another round.

Use crepe paper to make a giant graph of children's jumping distances. Put a piece of tape onto the end of a crepe-paper roll and hand the end to a child. Insert a pencil through the middle of the crepe-paper roll so that it will unwind easily. Hold both ends of the pencil and direct the child to jump with the end of the paper in his hand. Ask him to place the tape on the floor where he landed. Cut the strip from the roll and tape it down where you are standing. Move over a few inches and repeat the above procedure with a different child. Continue until each child has had a turn to jump; then compare the graph's results.

Encourage little ones to perfect their tying skills by practicing with crepe-paper streamers. Cut a supply of four-foot streamers. Invite students to tie bows around everything in sight—legs, waists, chairs, books, etc. Anything goes with bows!